Who's (H)Eating Earth?

Memes on Climate, Food & Hope

By

Moses Seenarine

Xpyr Press

Who's (H)Eating Earth? Memes on Climate, Food & Hope, published by Xpyr Press, Los Angeles, CA

xpyrpress.com

Cover and text design by myluv4earth
Printed and bound by Create Space, an Amazon Co.

Printed in the United States of America

ISBN-13: 978-0692739433

ISBN-10: 0692739432

Printed on recycled paper

Memes were designed by moses seenarine for various non-profit organizations, including Meat Climate Change (meatclimatechange.org), Climate Change 911 (CC911.net), 350.org, the Animal Advocacy Museum, and others. Art was inspired by the work of Favianna Rodriguez, Nohad Nassif, Lailati Nar, and many others.

Dedicated to nature, animals, women, children, public artists, and organic intellectuals everywhere.

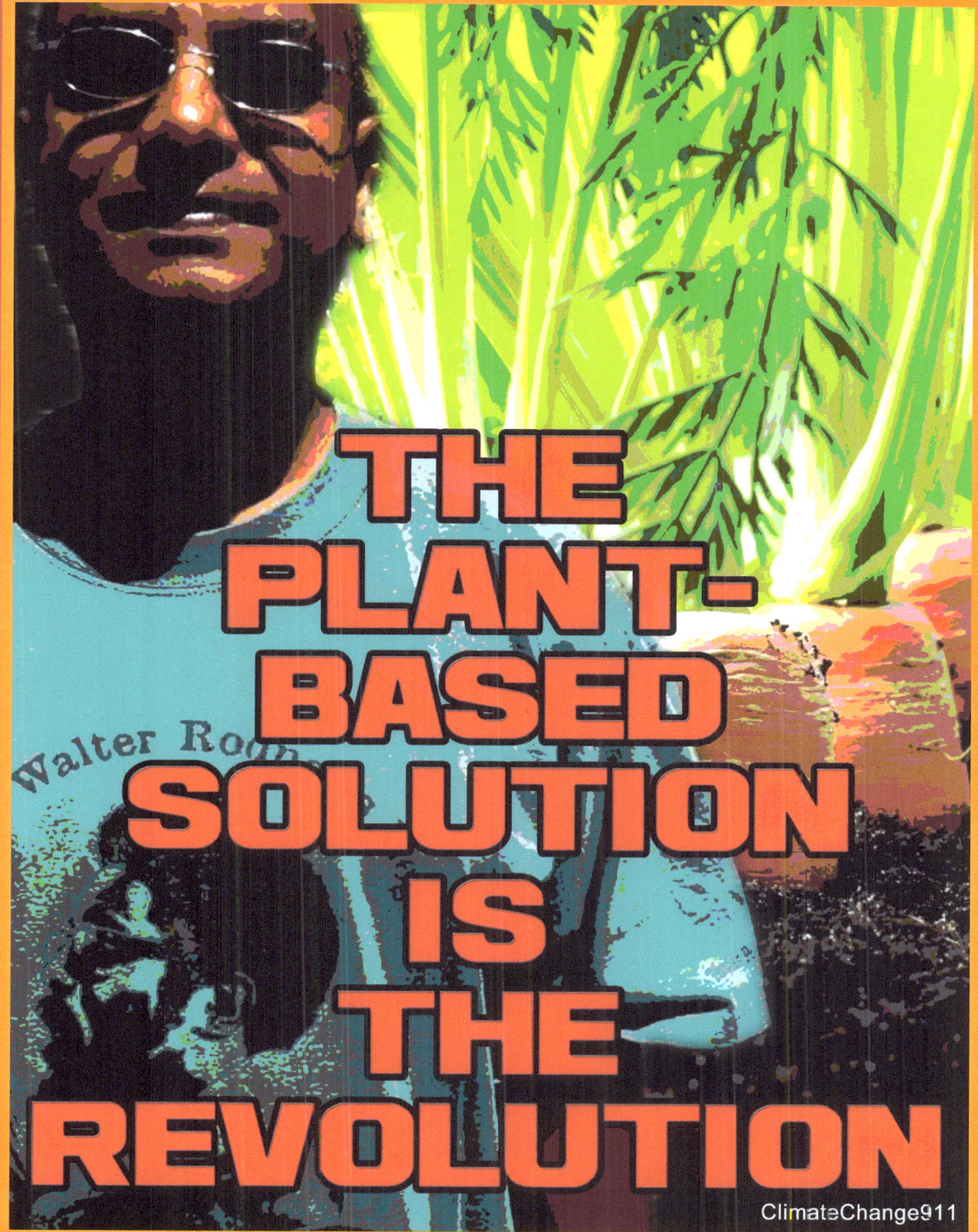

("*Plant-based Solution is the Revolution I*", digital media 2013)

Who's (H)Eating Earth? Memes on Climate, Food & Hope

2

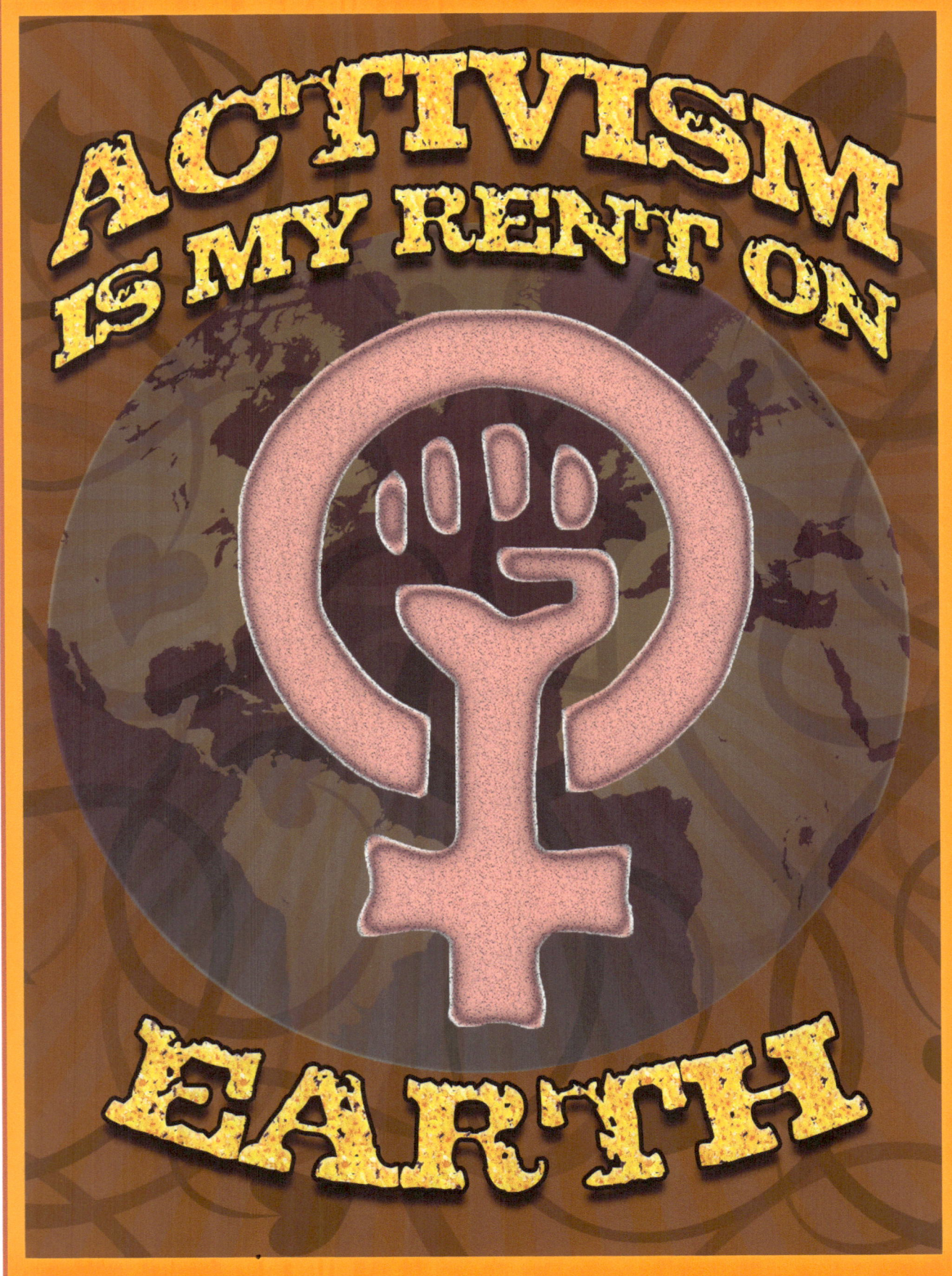

("*Activism is My Rent on Earth*", digital media 2012)

Who's (H)Eating Earth? Memes on Climate, Food & Hope

3

THERE ARE
MULTIPLE ROUTES TO
OVERALL CATASTROPHE

AND FEW
IF ANY ROUTES
TO ANYTHING ELSE

ClimateChange911

("*Multiple Routes to Catastrophe*", digital media 2013)

Who's (H)Eating Earth? Memes on Climate, Food & Hope

4

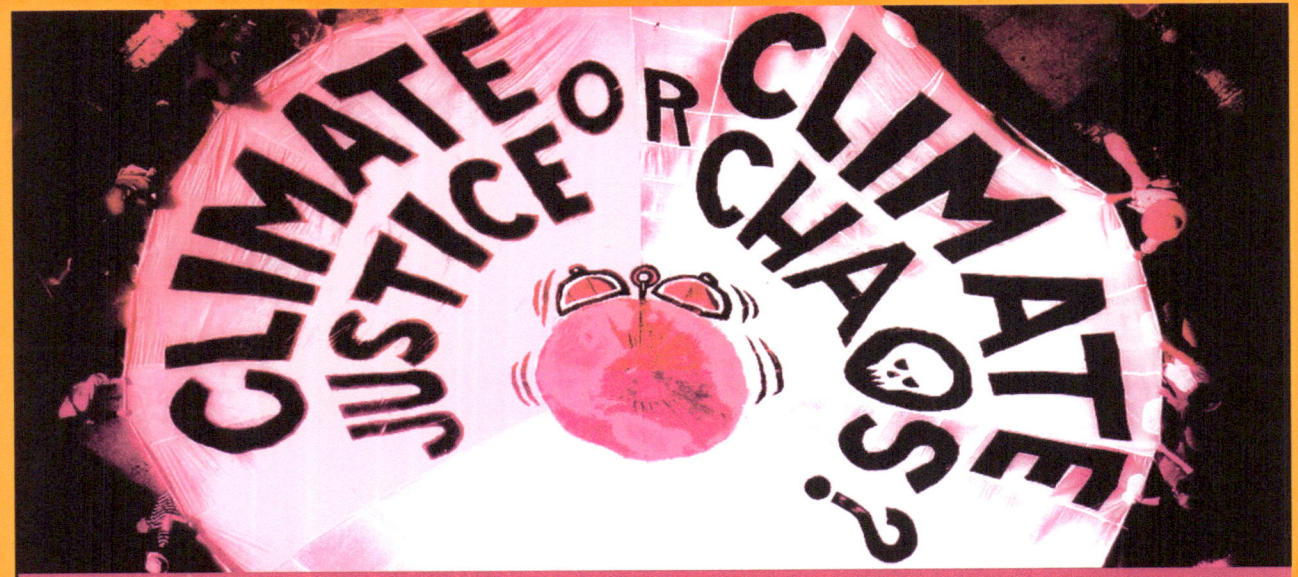

People's Climate March
SEPTEMBER 21, NYC

We must act together NOW to demand a world safe from the ravages of climate change!

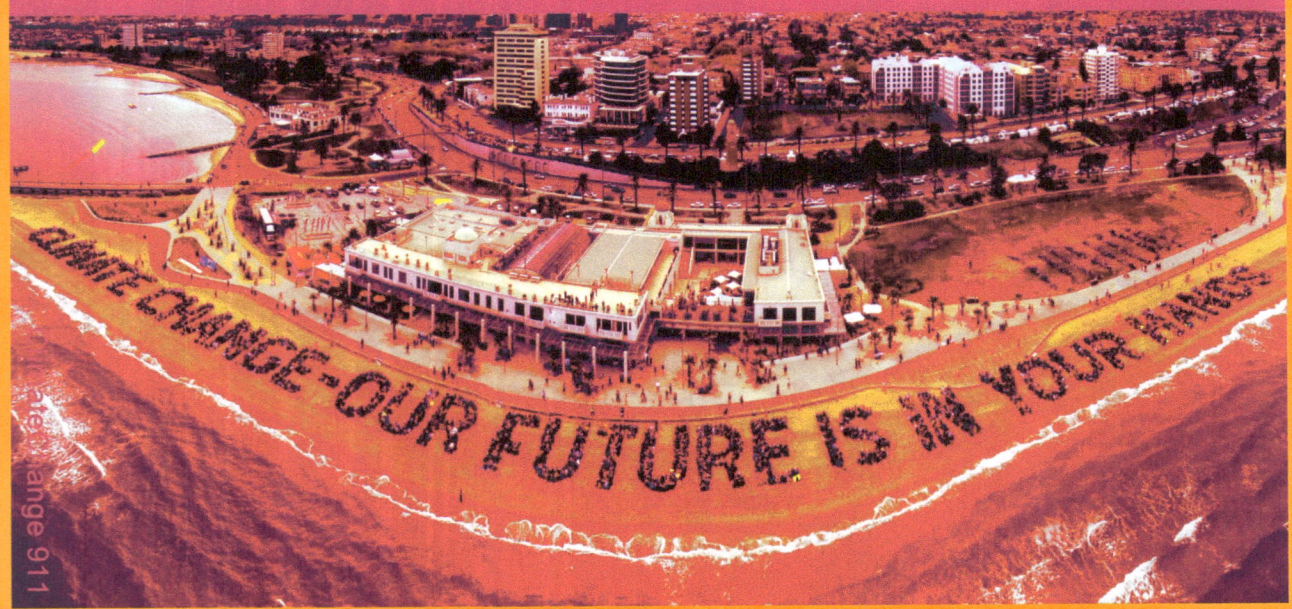

(*"People's Climate March I"*, digital media 2014)

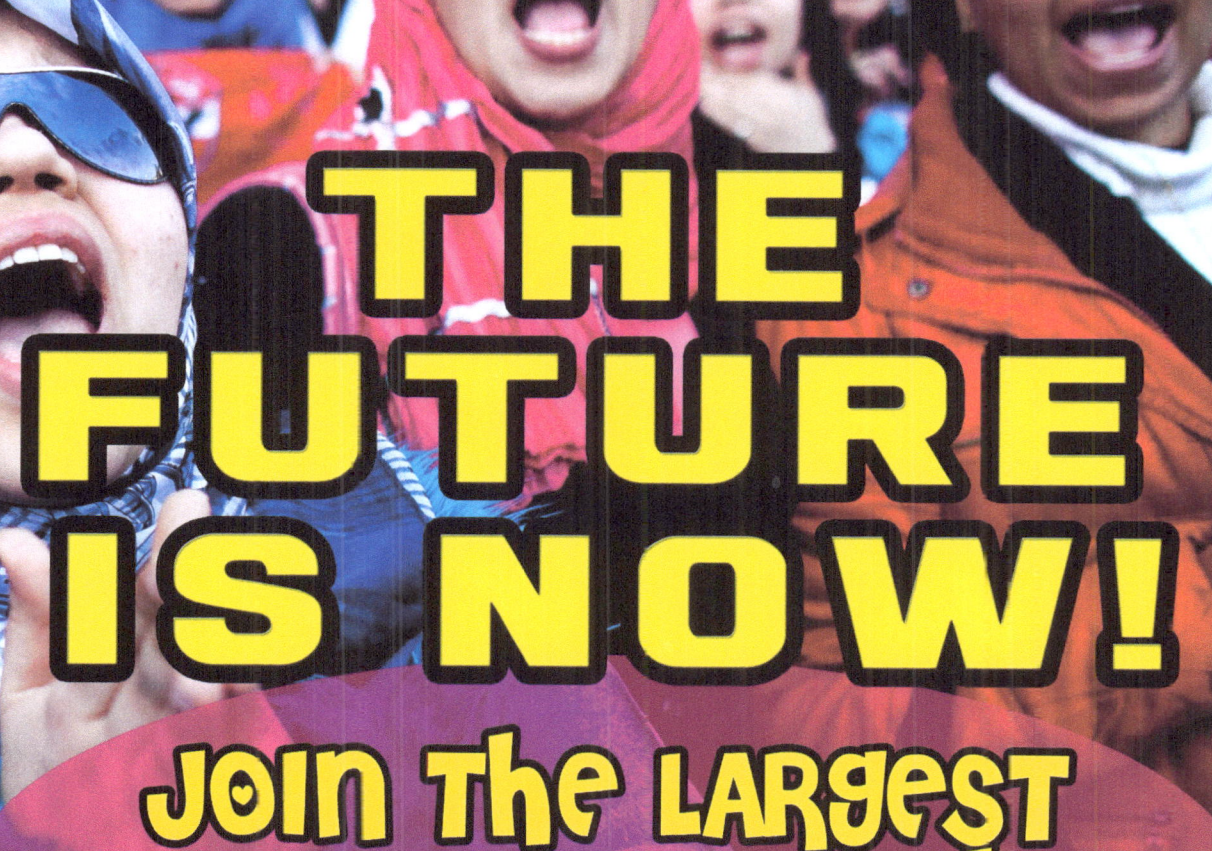

("People's Climate March II", digital media 2014)

Who's (H)Eating Earth? Memes on Climate, Food & Hope

6

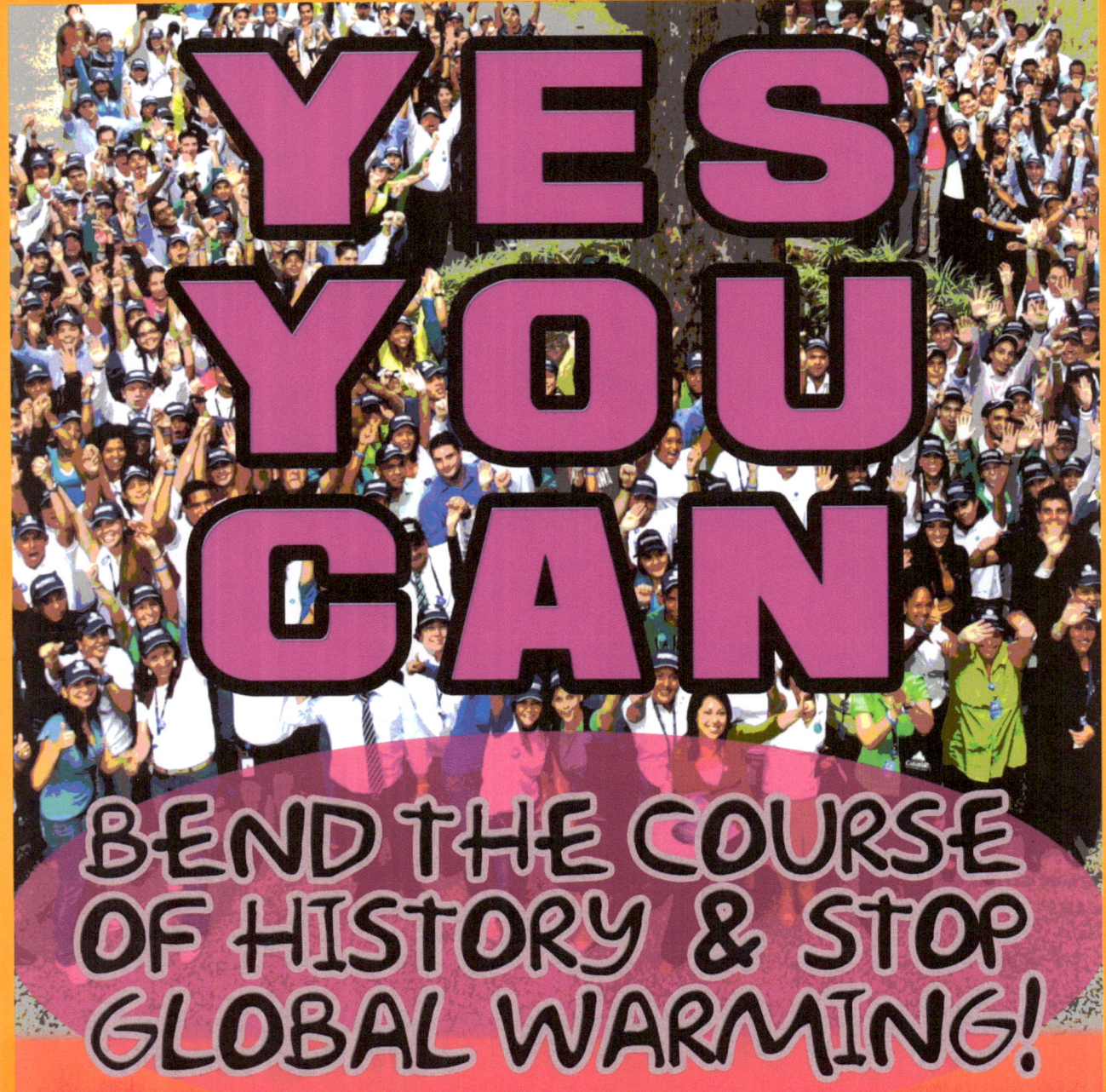

YES YOU CAN

BEND THE COURSE OF HISTORY & STOP GLOBAL WARMING!

Global Day of Action Sept. 20-21, 2014

ClimateChange911

("*People's Climate March III*", digital media 2014)

DURING THE LAST SEVEN YEARS WE'VE BROKEN PRETTY MUCH EVERY KIND OF WEATHER RECORD THERE IS, FROM HEAT TO TORNADOS TO FLOODS

Jeff Masters

ClimateChange911

(*"Broken Weather Records"*, digital media 2014)
Update: Weather records continue to fall

SINCE 1998 WE'VE HAD 10 OF 11 WARMEST YEARS ON RECORD WORLDWIDE

ClimateChange 911

("*Warmest Years on Record*", digital media 2014)

APRIL IS NOW THE FIRST MONTH IN RECORDED HISTORY IN WHICH CARBON DIOXIDE LEVELS EXCEEDED 400 PPM EVERY DAY

("*April's 400 ppm CO2 Milestone*", digital media 2014)

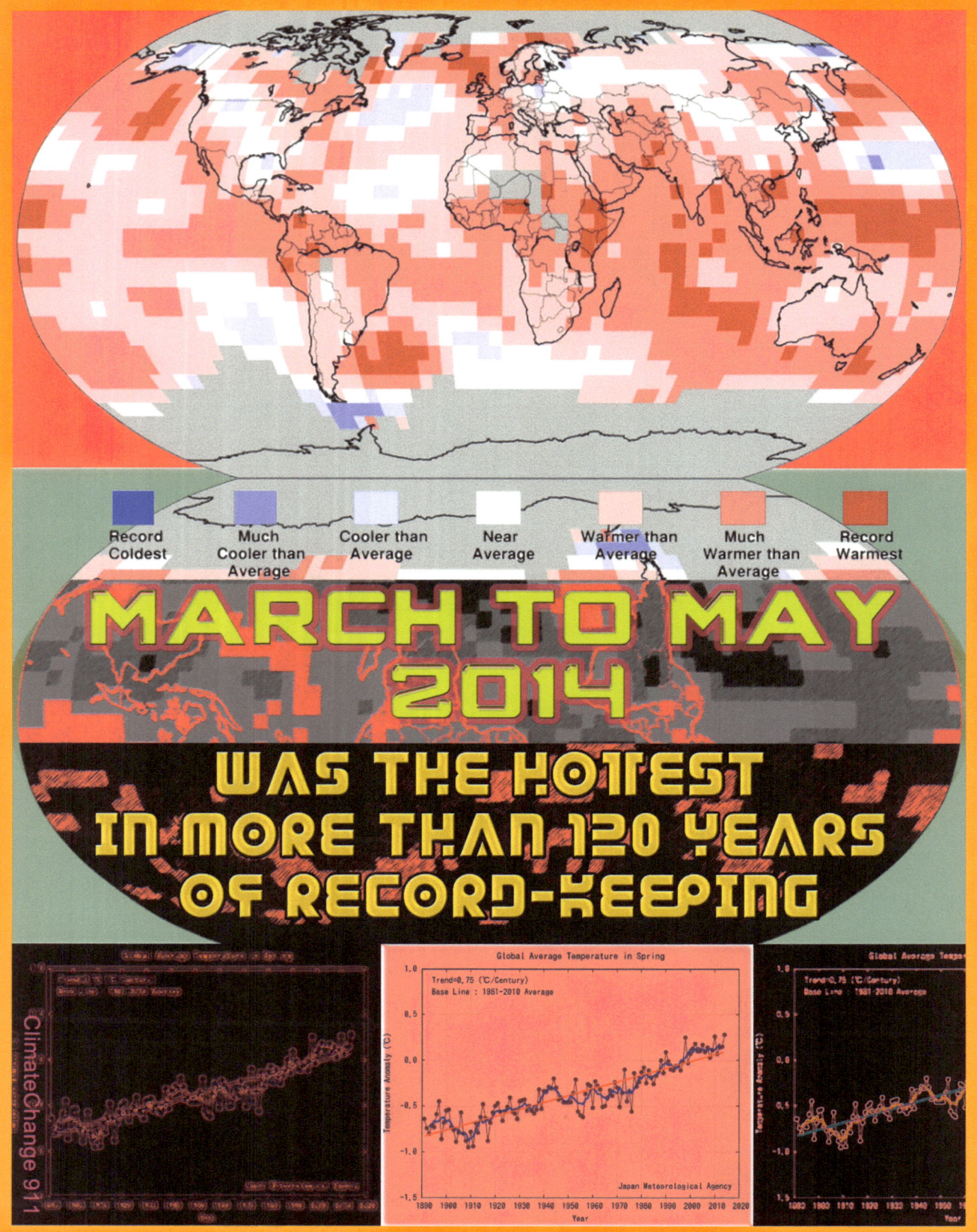

("***Three-Month Weather Record***", digital media 2014)
Update: 3-month record also broken in 2015 & 2016

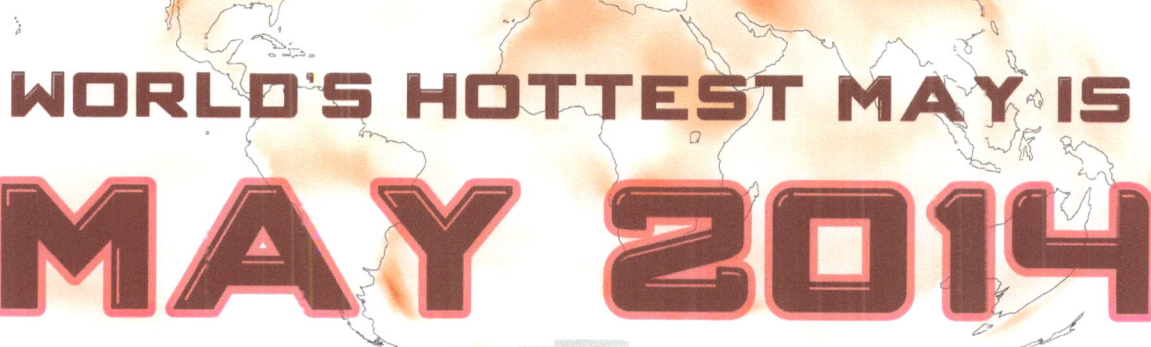

WORLD'S HOTTEST MAY IS
MAY 2014

ClimateChange 911

THE COMBINED AVERAGE TEMPERATURE OVER GLOBAL LAND AND OCEAN SURFACES WAS RECORD HIGHEST FOR THIS MONTH AT 0.74°C (1.33°F) ABOVE THE 20TH CENTURY AVERAGE OF 14.8°C (58.6°F)

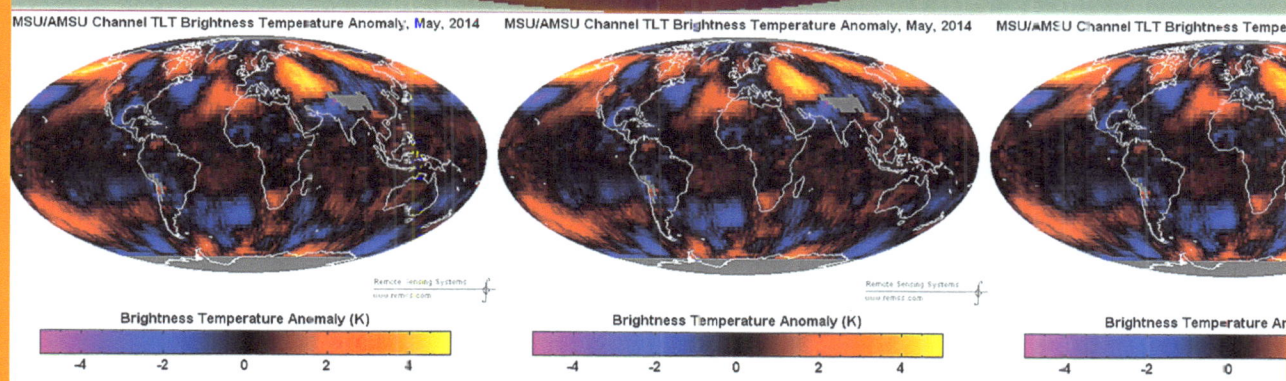

("***Hottest May***", digital media 2014)
Update: Record Mays in 2015 & 2016

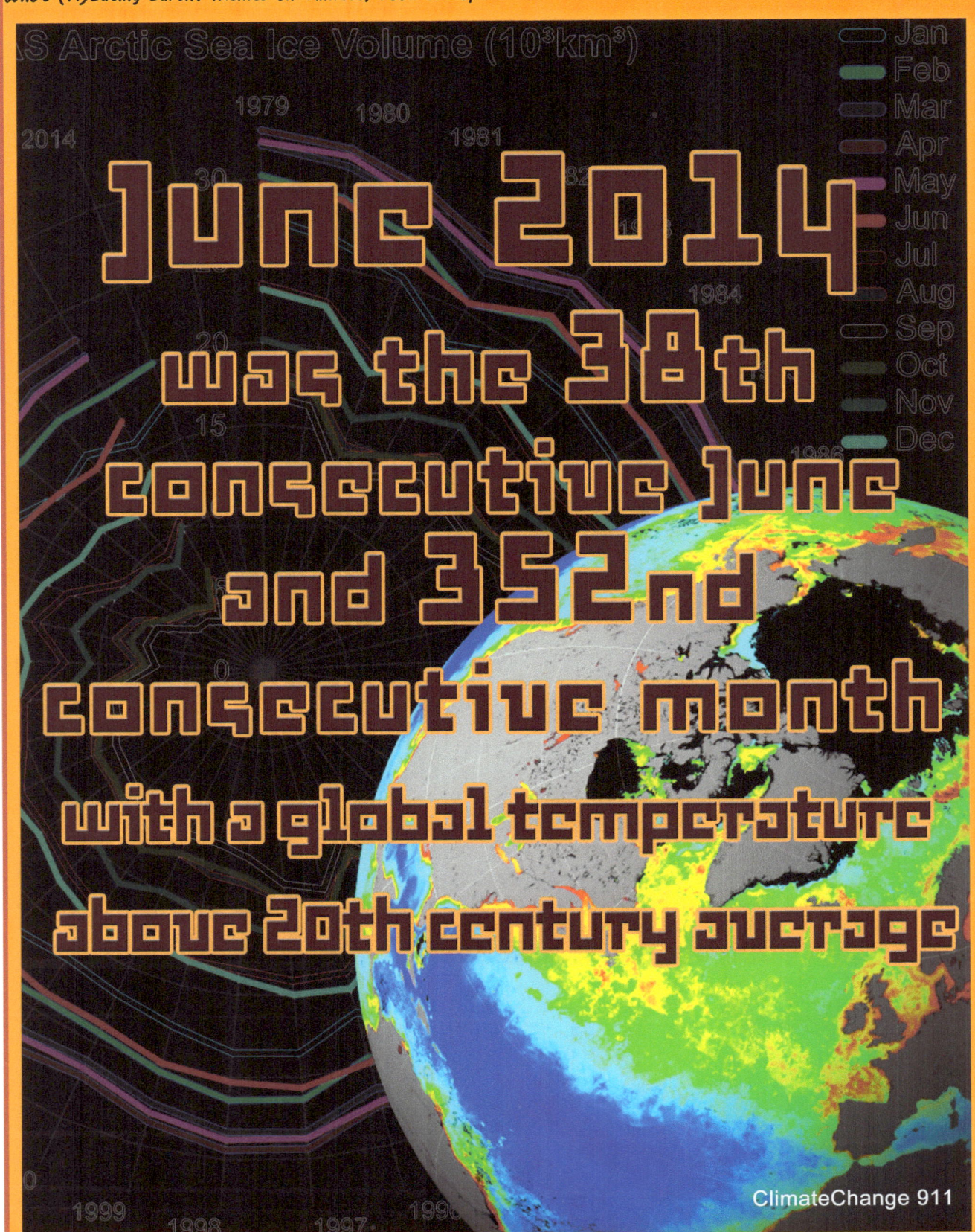

June 2014 was the 38th consecutive June and 352nd consecutive month with a global temperature above 20th century average

ClimateChange 911

("*352-Month Record*", digital media 2014)
Update: Temperature trend remains unbroken

Climate Change By the Numbers

97% - How certain scientists now are that human activity has caused at least half of climate change in the last half-century.

90% - How certain scientists were that human activity has caused at least half of climate change in the last half-century in 2007.

7 to 23 inches - The projected amount sea levels were expected to rise by the end of the century in 2007.

10 to 32 inches - The projected amount sea levels are now expected to rise by the end of the century.

0.5 to 8.6 degrees - How much average global temperatures are now expected to rise by the end of the century.

56.4 degrees - The average global temperature in 1850.

58.2 degrees - The average global temperature in 2012.

40 percent - The percentage rise in the concentration of carbon dioxide in the atmosphere between the years 1750 and 2011.

2,000,000,000,000 - The tonnes of carbon dioxide added to the atmosphere from fossil fuel burning, cement production, deforestation and land clearing between 1750 and 2011.

275,000,000,000 - The amount of ice in tonnes per year which "very likely" melted from the world's glaciers between 1993 and 2009

90% - The percentage of extra energy in the climate system between 1971 and 2010 that has been taken up by warming oceans.

20 years - The average period of time weather catastrophes, like Superstorm Sandy, are now expected to strike. Previously, these were called "storms of the century."

(*Climate Change by the Numbers*", digital media 2014)

US Climate Change 2014

1. 2001-2012 was the warmest on record globally. Every year was warmer than the 1990s average.
2. The sun's output has not varied substantially as temperatures have risen.
3. U.S. temperatures have warmed 1.3 - 1.9 degrees since 1895, with most of the increase since 1970.
4. Precipitation events are trending heavier in the U.S.
5. Sea levels are rising, with some of the fastest rates (1-2 feet per century) in the Northeast.
6. Warmer ocean temperatures are leading to an increase in coral bleaching in tropical areas.
7. The length of the frost-free season is growing.
8. The ragweed (pollen) season is expanding.
9. Heating demand is decreasing, cooling demand is increasing.
10. Temperatures are projected to warm from a few to over 10 degrees by 2100.
11. The hottest days are projected to warm substantially.
12. Sea levels in the U.S. are projected to rise 1 to 4 feet.
13. Warming is projected to reduce soil moisture in much of the West by several to 10 - 15% by 2100.
14. The projected increase in the frost-free season, days without precipitation and hot nights will impact agriculture.
15. Climate change significantly increases the risk of water supply stress by mid-century, especially in the western U.S.

ClimateChange 911

("*US Climate Change 2014*", digital media 2014)

BY 2020, THE UNITED STATES IS PROJECTED TO BECOME THE LARGEST GLOBAL OIL PRODUCER.

AND WITH THE SHALE PRODUCTION IN THE US & TAR SANDS IN CANADA, NORTH AMERICA BECOMES A NET OIL EXPORTER AROUND 2030.

IEA World Energy Outlook 2012

THE US WANTS TO SELL OIL TO THE REST OF THE WORLD NOT KEEP IT IN THE GROUND AND SOLVE THE CLIMATE CRISIS!

ClimateChange911

("*U.S. of Oil*", digital media 2013)

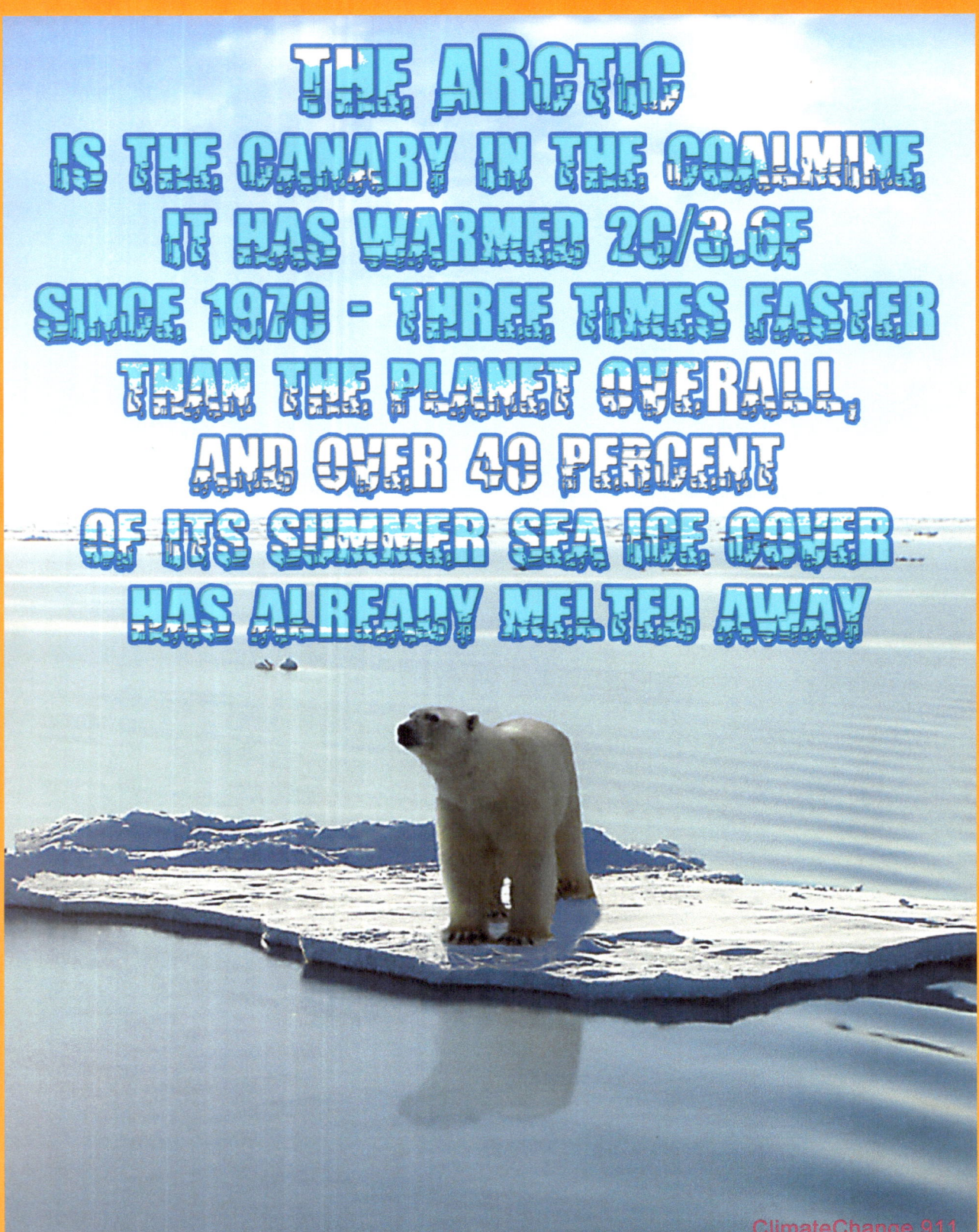

THE ARCTIC IS THE CANARY IN THE COALMINE IT HAS WARMED 2C/3.6F SINCE 1970 - THREE TIMES FASTER THAN THE PLANET OVERALL, AND OVER 40 PERCENT OF ITS SUMMER SEA ICE COVER HAS ALREADY MELTED AWAY

ClimateChange 911

("*Arctic Canary*", digital media 2013)

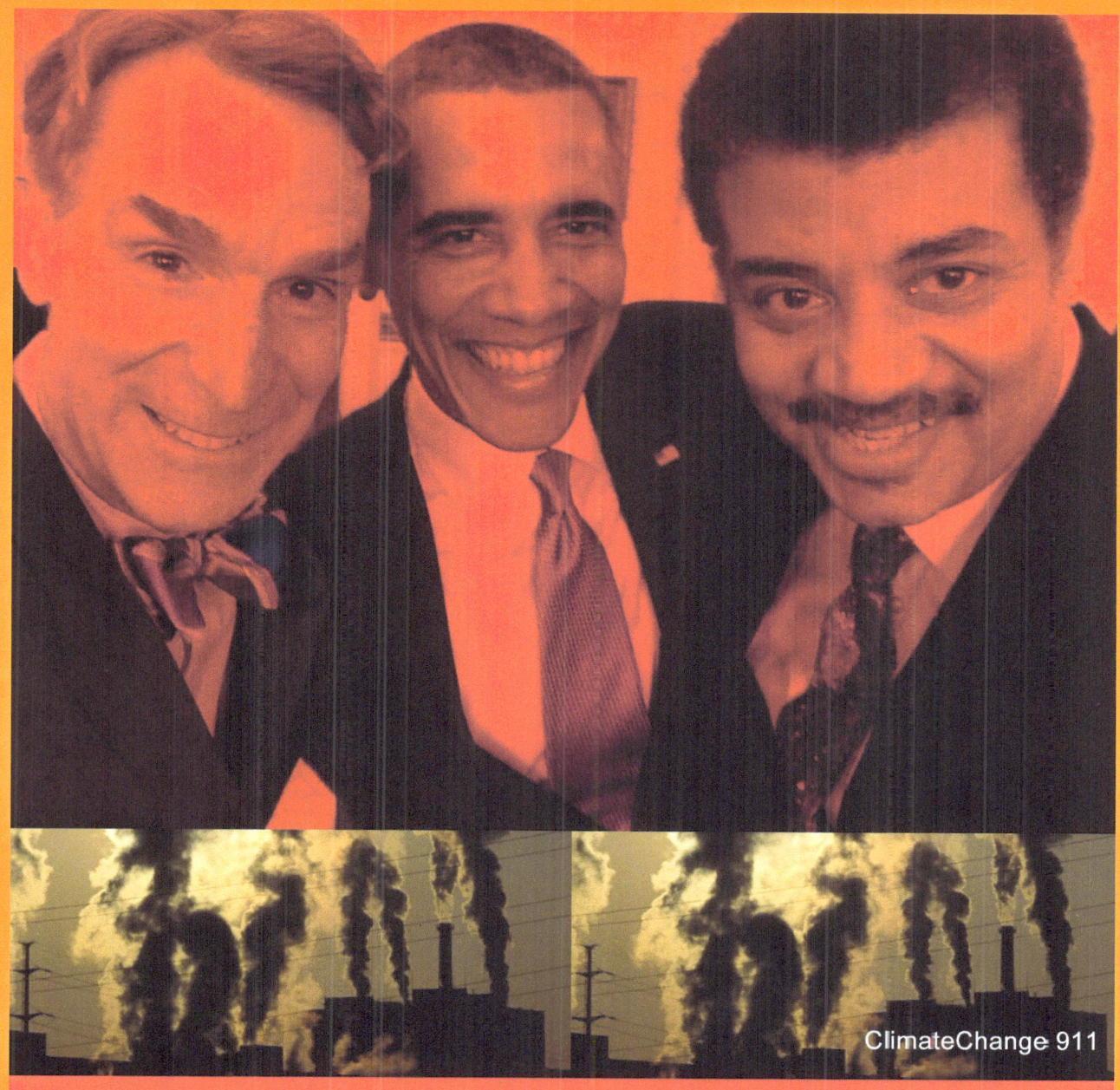

IF SCIENTISTS DO NOT STEP OUT OF THEIR COMFORT ZONES AND TAKE A MORE VOCAL STAND, THEY FACE THE RISK OF BECOMING IRRELEVANT TO SOCIETY AS THE RAPID RAMPING UP OF EXTREME WEATHER EVENTS, FOOD SHORTAGES, AND GLOBAL TURMOIL SWEEPS ALL LOGIC AND RATIONALITY ASIDE.

- Paul Beckwith

("*Irrelevant Scientists*", digital media 2014)

Who's (H)Eating Earth? Memes on Climate, Food & Hope

18

"IF THE WORLD KEEPS BURNING FOSSIL FUELS AT THE CURRENT RATE, IT WILL CROSS A THRESHOLD INTO ENVIRONMENTAL RUIN BY 2036"

Michael E. Mann

("2036 Threshold to Ruin", digital media 2014)

Who's (H)Eating Earth? Memes on Climate, Food & Hope

19

In the next 40 years climate change could commit over a third of all species to extinction

ClimateChange911

("*Extinction of 1/3 of Species*", digital media 2013)

Who's (H)Eating Earth? Memes on Climate, Food & Hope

20

"IF CIVILIZATION DOES NOT COLLAPSE QUICKLY THIS CENTURY, THEN CO2 LEVELS WILL LIKELY END UP EXCEEDING 1000 PPMV; BUT, IF CO2 LEVELS RISE BY THIS MUCH, THEN THE RISK IS THAT CIVILIZATION WILL GRADUALLY TEND TOWARDS COLLAPSE."

- T. J. Garrett

ClimateChange911

("*End-Civ or Civ-End?*", digital media 2014)

"UNTIL RECENTLY THE SCALE OF THE PERMIAN MASS EXTINCTION WAS SEEN AS JUST TOO MASSIVE, ITS DURATION FAR TOO LONG, AND DATING TOO IMPRECISE FOR A SENSIBLE COMPARISON TO BE MADE WITH TODAY'S CLIMATE CHANGE. NO LONGER."

- Skeptical Science
02042014

ClimateChange911

(*"Permian Now!"*, digital media 2014)

THE MOST RELIABLE INDICATOR OF HUMAN ARRIVAL IN THE FOSSIL RECORD IS A WAVE OF LARGE MAMMAL EXTINCTIONS

Todd Surovell
Archaeologist

ClimateChange911

(*Precedent to 6th Mass Extinction*, digital media 2014)

"HUMANS HAVE TINKERED WITH THE NATURAL WORLD SINCE WE APPEARED ON THE EVOLUTIONARY STAGE. OUR DAYS MAY BE NUMBERED. AS THE HOME TEAM. NATURE BATS LAST."

- Guy McPherson

ClimateChange911

("*Nature Bats Last*", digital media 2013)

TEMPERATURE PROJECTIONS

* Late 2007: 1C increase by 2100. (IPCC)

* Late 2008: 2C increase by 2100.
(The Hadley Centre for Meteorological Research)

* Mid-2009: 3.5C increase by 2100.
(The U.N. Environment Programme)

* Oct 2009: 4C increase by 2060.
(The Hadley Centre for Meteorological Research)

* Nov 2009: 6C - 7C increase by 2100.
(The Global Carbon Project)

* Dec 2010: 5C increase by 2050.
(The U.N. Environment Programme)

* 2012: On track to 2C increase by 2017. (IEA)

* Nov 2013: 3.5C increase by 2035. (IEA)

Humans have never lived on a planet at 3.5C above baseline. Such an increase would remove habitat for human beings on this planet, as nearly all the plankton in the oceans would be destroyed, and associated temperature swings would kill off many land plants.

ClimateChange 911

("*Temperature Projections*", digital media 2014)

Who's (H)Eating Earth? Memes on Climate, Food & Hope

25

We have to control methane immediately,

and natural gas is the largest methane

pollution source in the United States.

If we hit a climate-system tipping point

because of methane,

our carbon dioxide problem is immaterial.

We have to get a handle on methane,

or increasingly risk global catastrophe."

Robert Howarth

("*Methane Crisis*", digital media 2014)

Biodiversity and Ecosystems are under threat from Climate Change, AND their Preservation and Restoration are crucial to Mitigating, Adapting to and even Reversing Climate Change

ClimateChange911

("*Biodiversity Matters*", digital media 2013)

Even though
the primary responsibility
of the North
to reduce emissions
has been recognized
in the UN,
the production
and consumption habits
of industrialized countries
like the United States
continue to threaten
the survival of humanity
and biodiversity globally

Climate Change 911

("*Over-consumption Crisis*", digital media 2013)

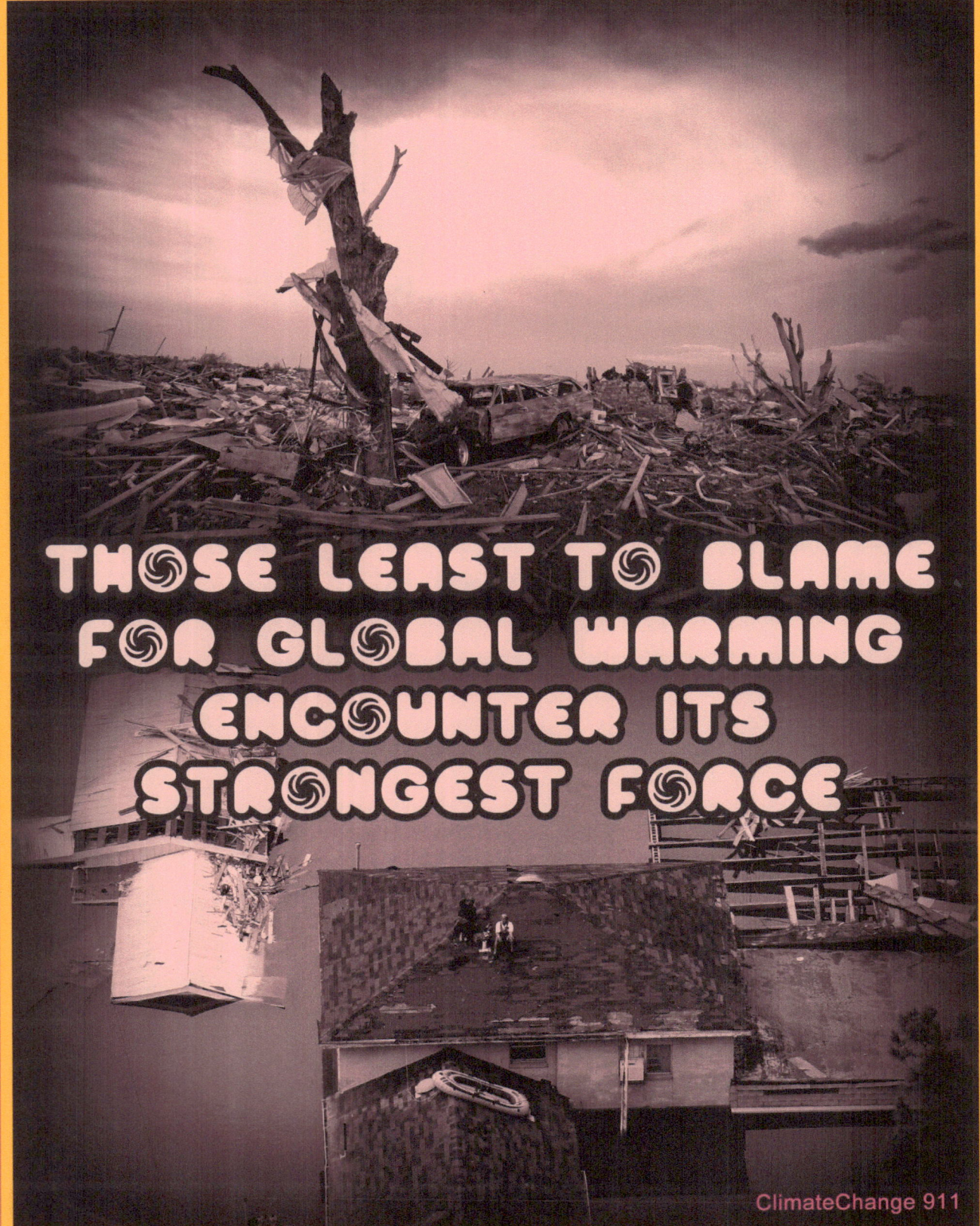

THOSE LEAST TO BLAME FOR GLOBAL WARMING ENCOUNTER ITS STRONGEST FORCE

ClimateChange 911

("*Least to Blame*", digital media 2013)

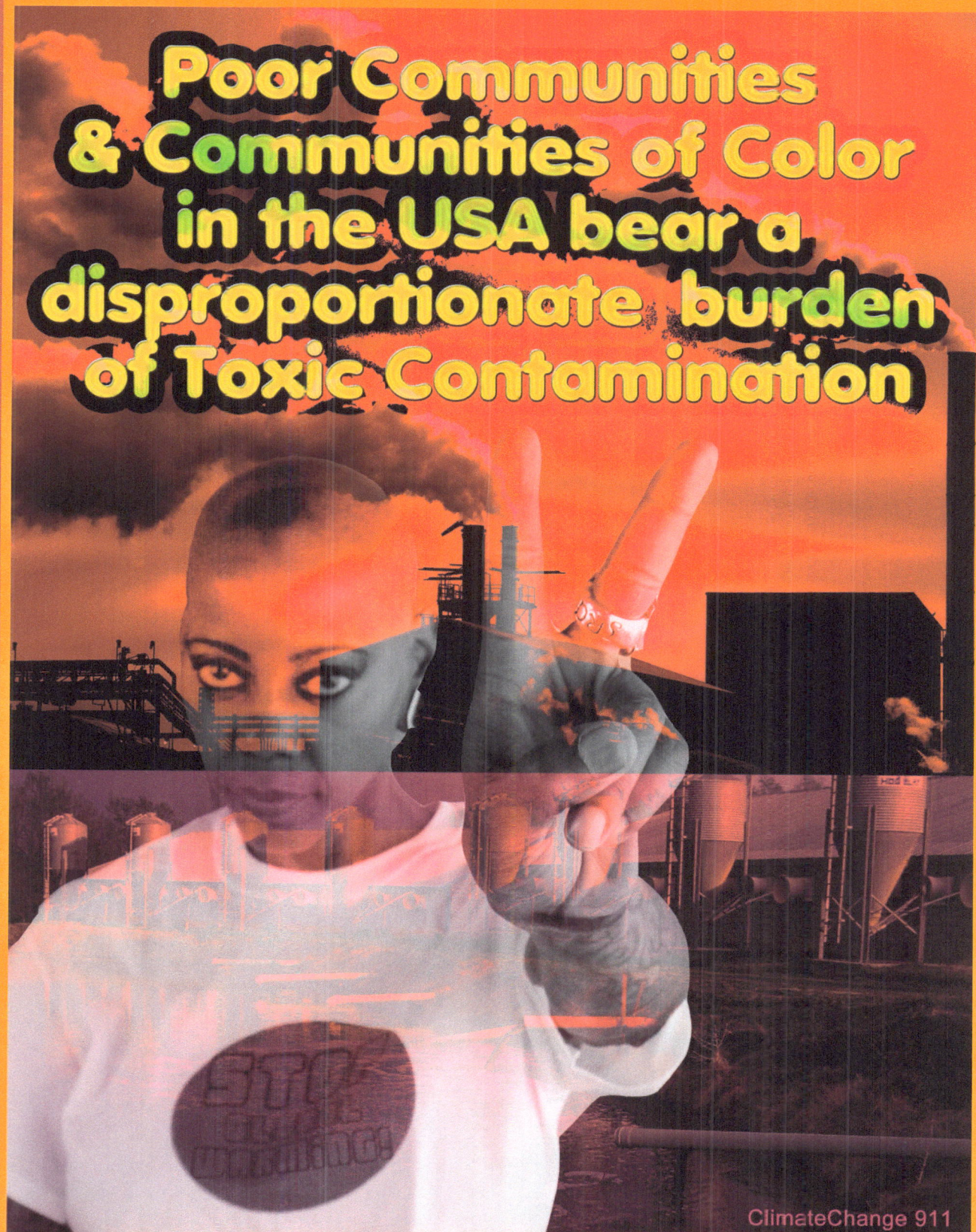

("**Disproportionate Burden**", digital media, model: Debra Wilson, 2019)

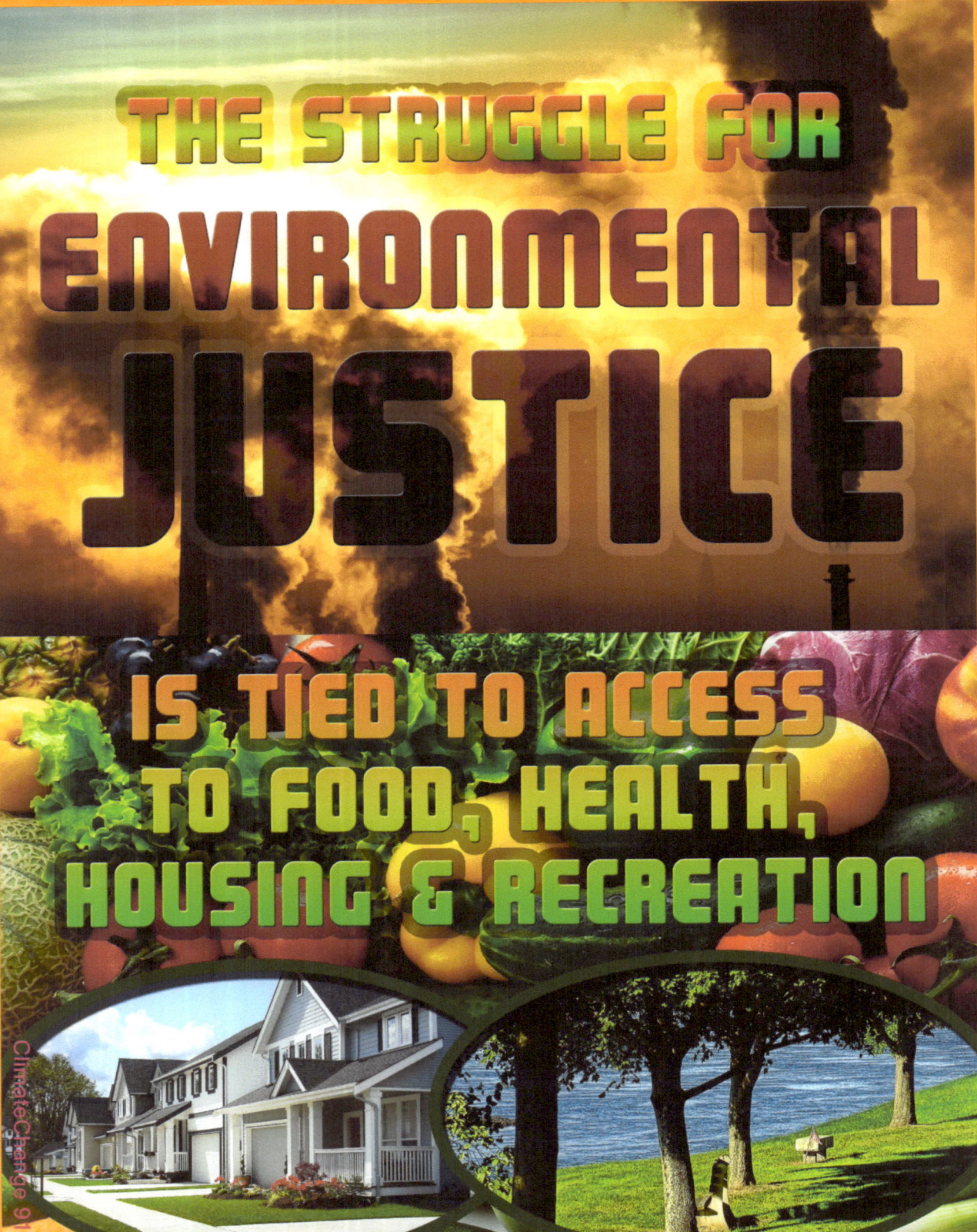

("*Environmental Justice I*", digital media 2013)

Who's (H)Eating Earth? Memes on Climate, Food & Hope

37

Principles for Climate Justice

- **Leave Fossil Fuels in the Ground**
- **Demand Real and Effective Solutions**
- **Industrialized Developed Countries Take Responsibility**
- **Living in a Good Way on Mother Earth**

Indigenous Environmental Network

COPYRIGHT 1898
F. A. RINEHART,
OMAHA

THUNDER CLOUD
— BLACKFEET —
Climate Change 911
No. 1385

(*"Environmental Justice II"*, digital media 2013)

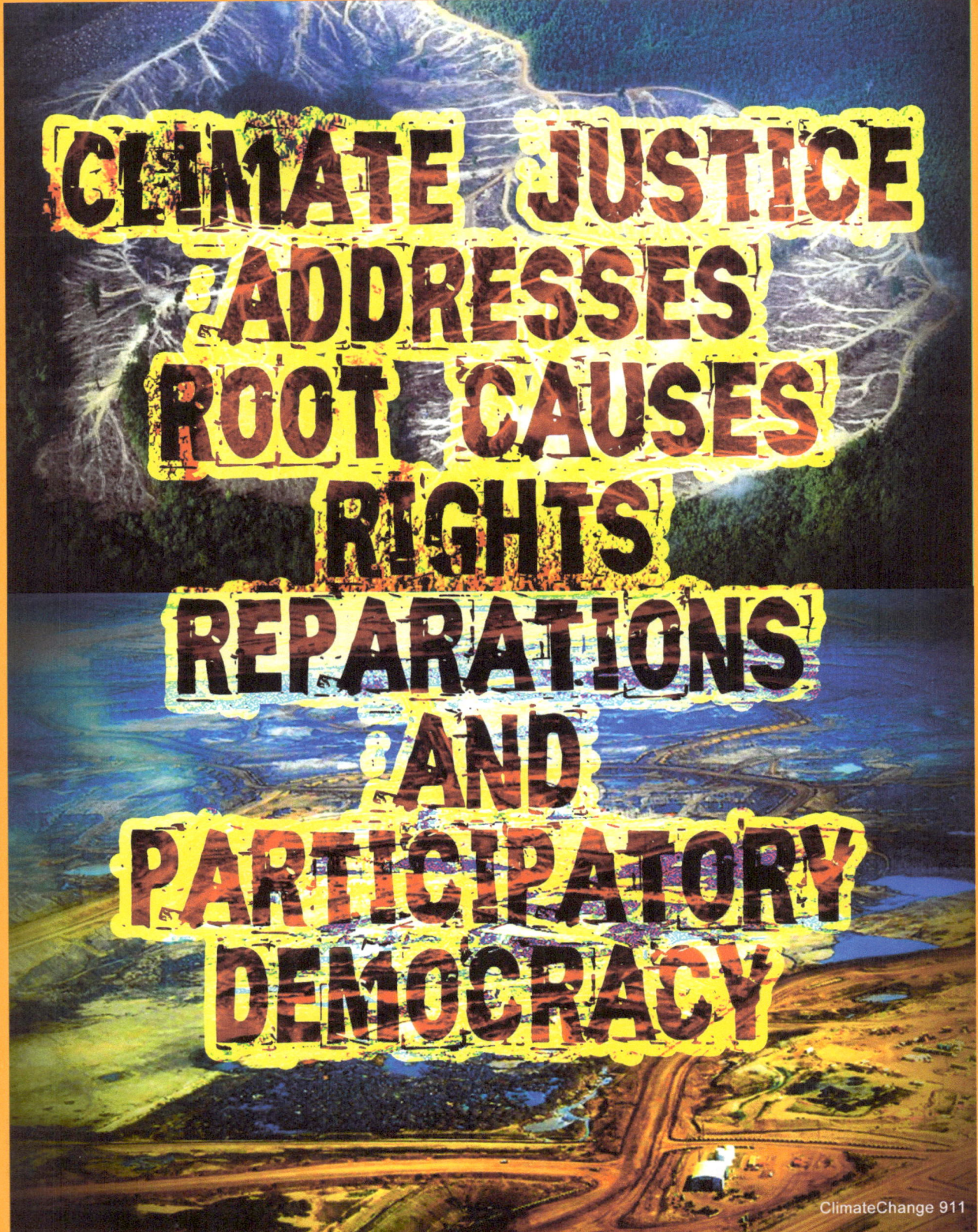

CLIMATE JUSTICE ADDRESSES ROOT CAUSES RIGHTS REPARATIONS AND PARTICIPATORY DEMOCRACY

ClimateChange 911

(*Environmental Justice III*, digital media 2013)

Food Justice!
Fair Wage / Fair Trade

POOR COMMUNITIES LIVE IN NUTRITIONAL DESERTS

Fast Food = Fast Death

("*Food Justice*", digital media 2013)

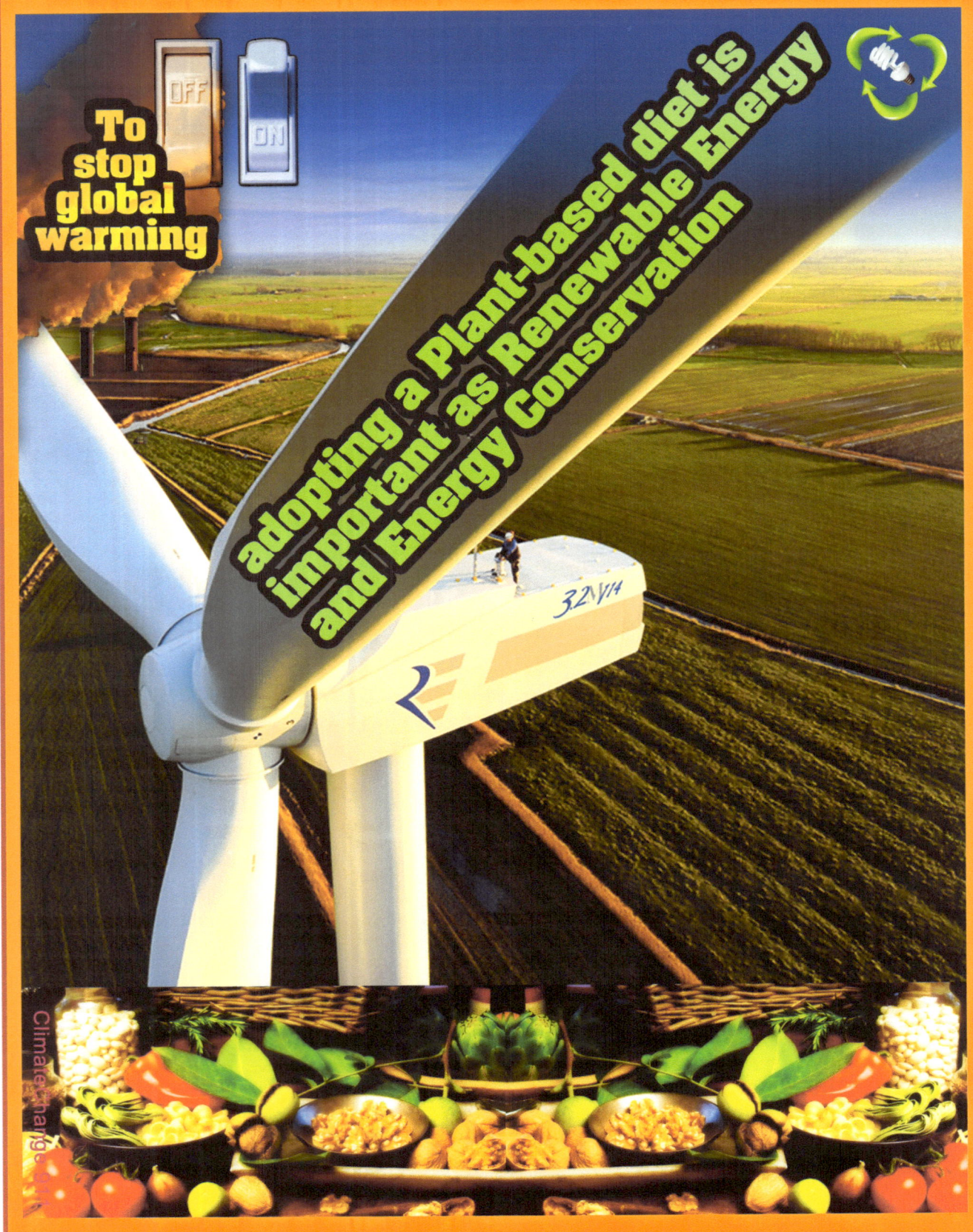

("*Two Alternatives Necessary*", digital media 2013)

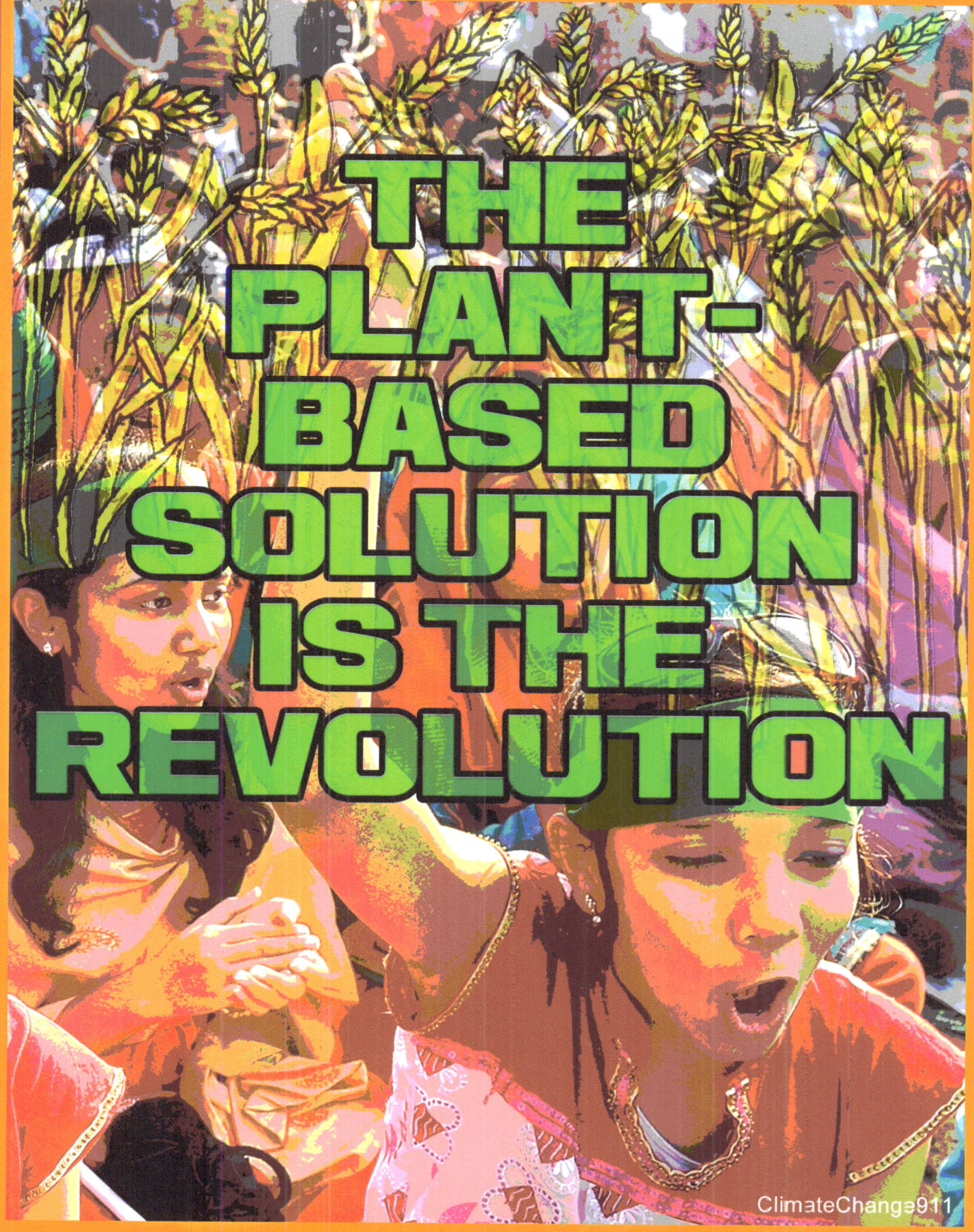

("*Plant-based Solution is the Revolution II*", digital media 2013)

Who's (H)Eating Earth? Memes on Climate, Food & Hope

36

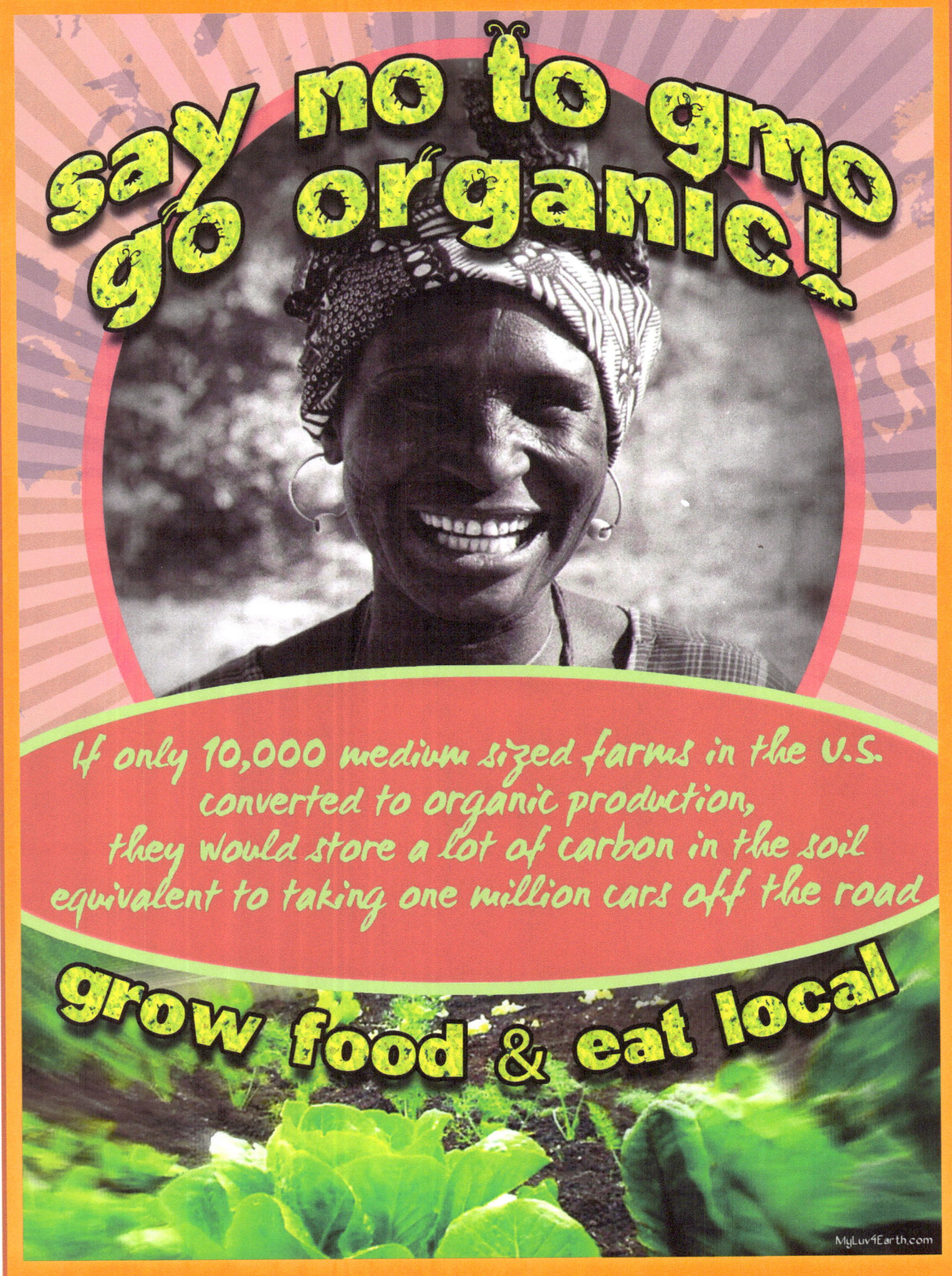

("*Go Organic*", digital media 2013)

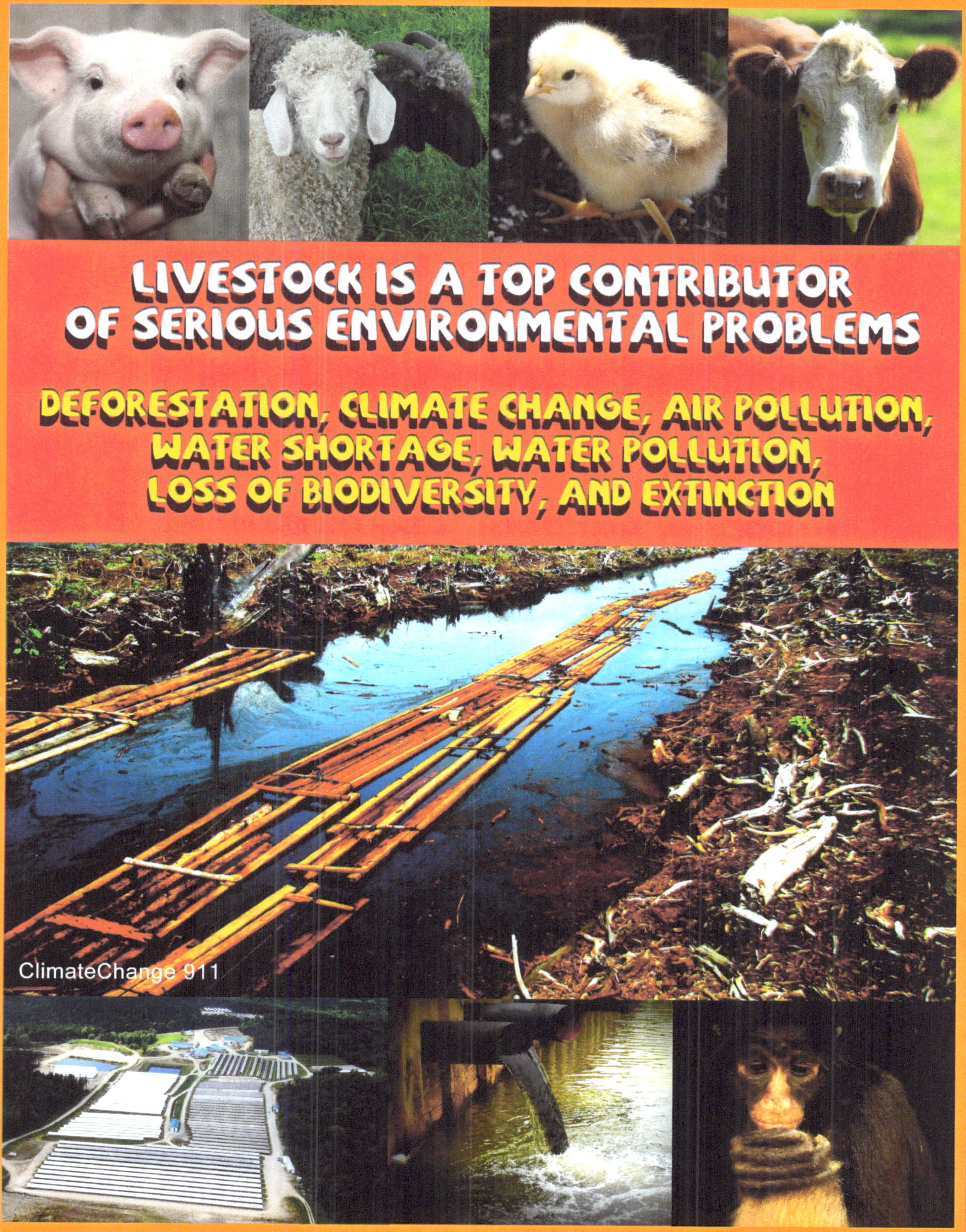

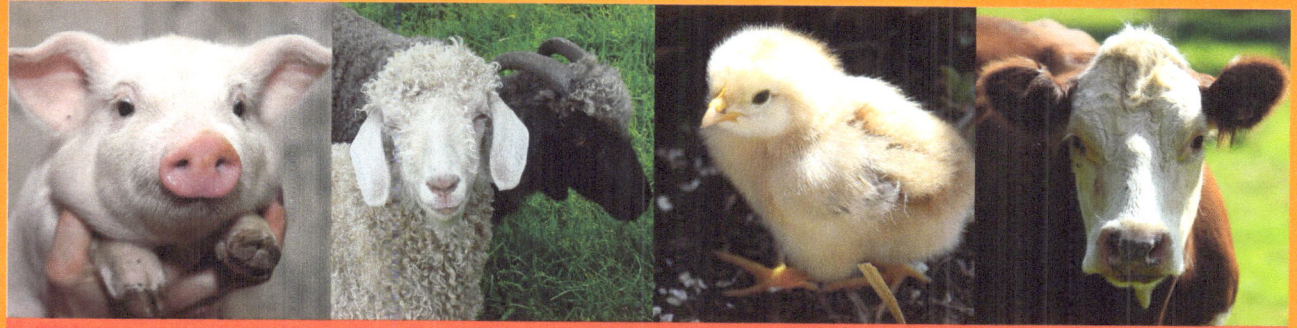

LIVESTOCK IS A TOP CONTRIBUTOR OF SERIOUS ENVIRONMENTAL PROBLEMS

DEFORESTATION, CLIMATE CHANGE, AIR POLLUTION, WATER SHORTAGE, WATER POLLUTION, LOSS OF BIODIVERSITY, AND EXTINCTION

("*Impact of Farmed Animals I*", digital media 2013)

Who's (H)Eating Earth? Memes on Climate, Food & Hope

38

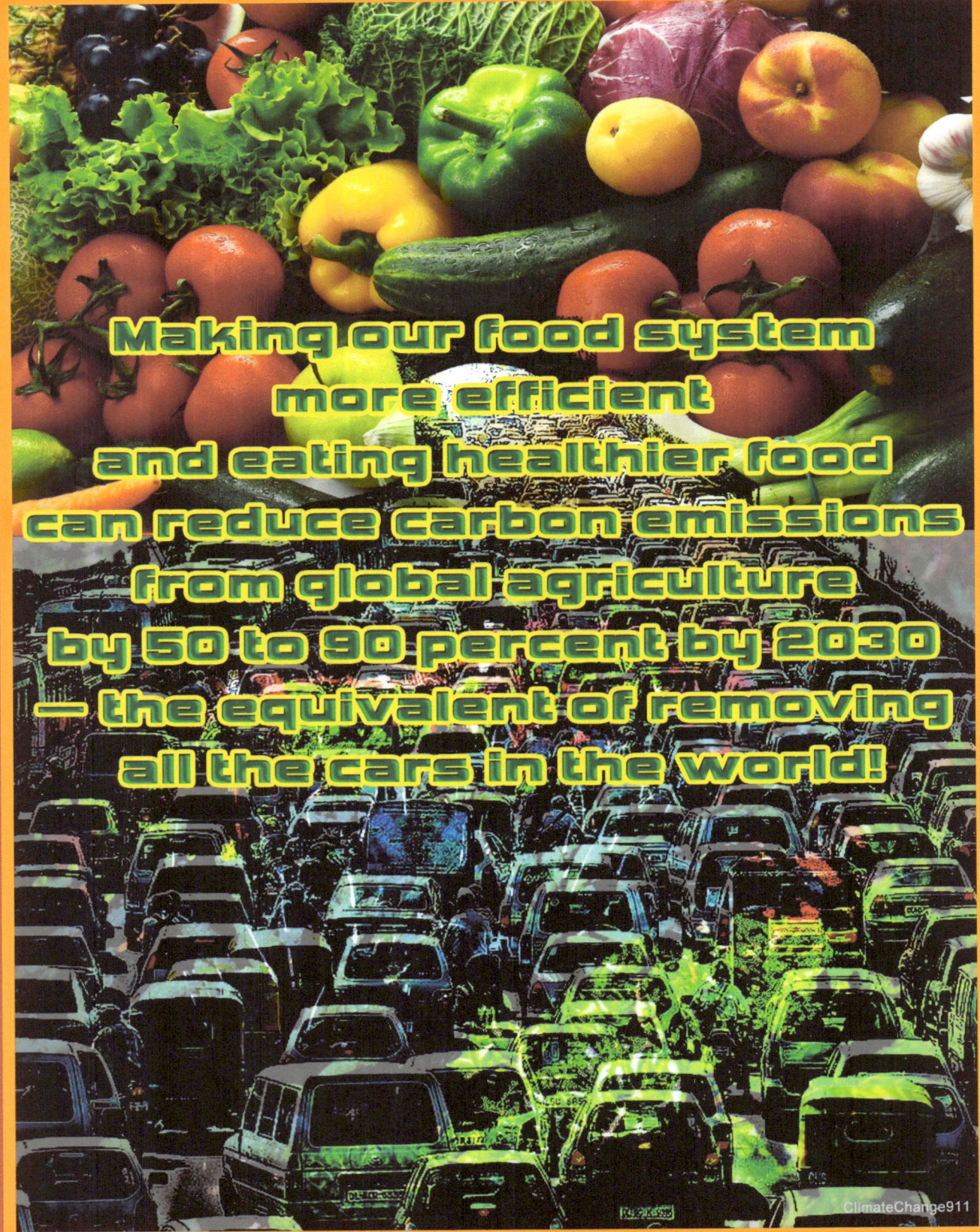

Making our food system
more efficient
and eating healthier food
can reduce carbon emissions
from global agriculture
by 50 to 90 percent by 2030
— the equivalent of removing
all the cars in the world!

ClimateChange911

(*"Eating Healthy is Like Removing All Cars"*, digital media 2013)

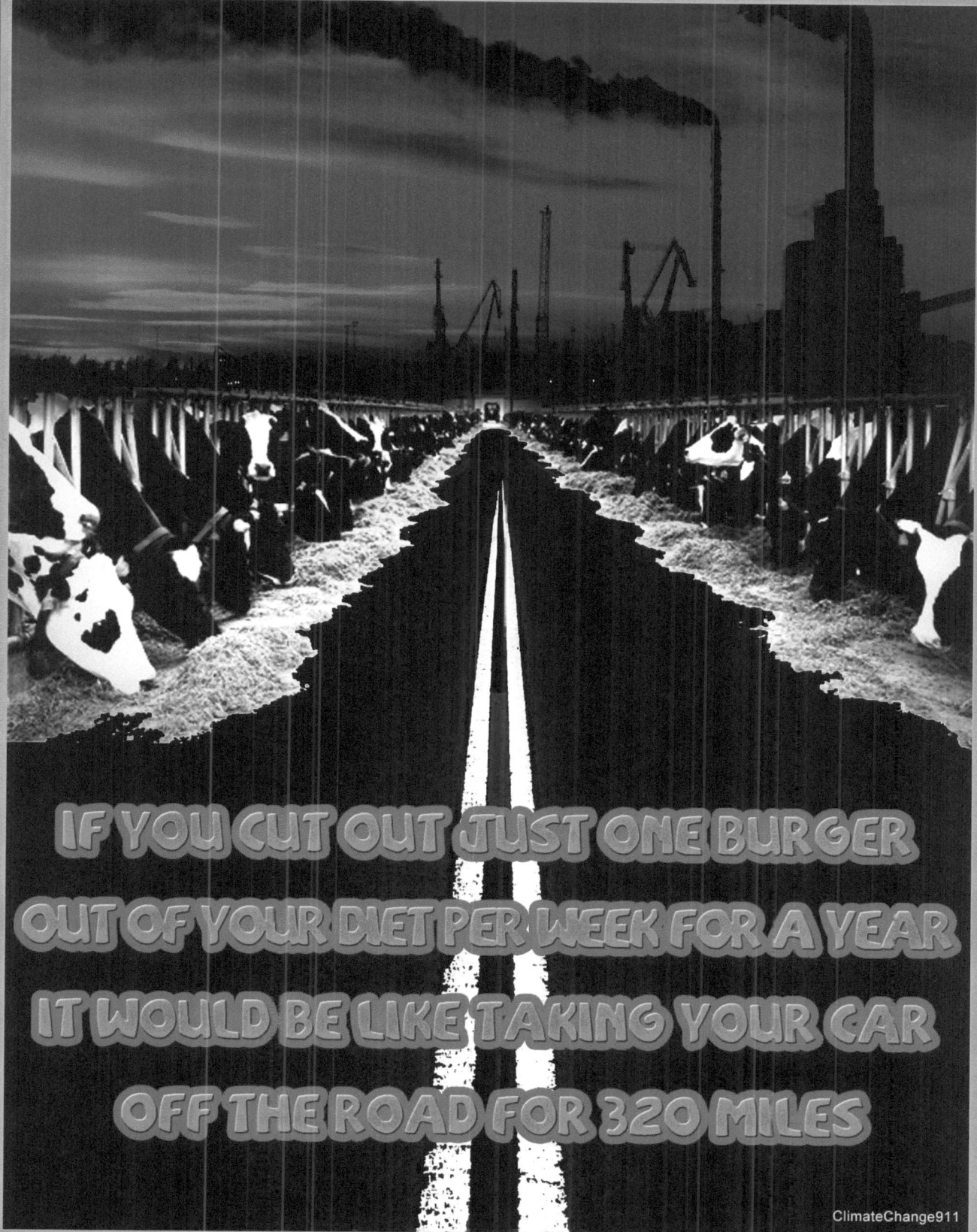

IF YOU CUT OUT JUST ONE BURGER OUT OF YOUR DIET PER WEEK FOR A YEAR IT WOULD BE LIKE TAKING YOUR CAR OFF THE ROAD FOR 320 MILES

ClimateChange911

("*Eat 1 Less Burger & Save 320 Miles Per Year*", digital media 2013)

Who's (H)Eating Earth? Memes on Climate, Food & Hope

40

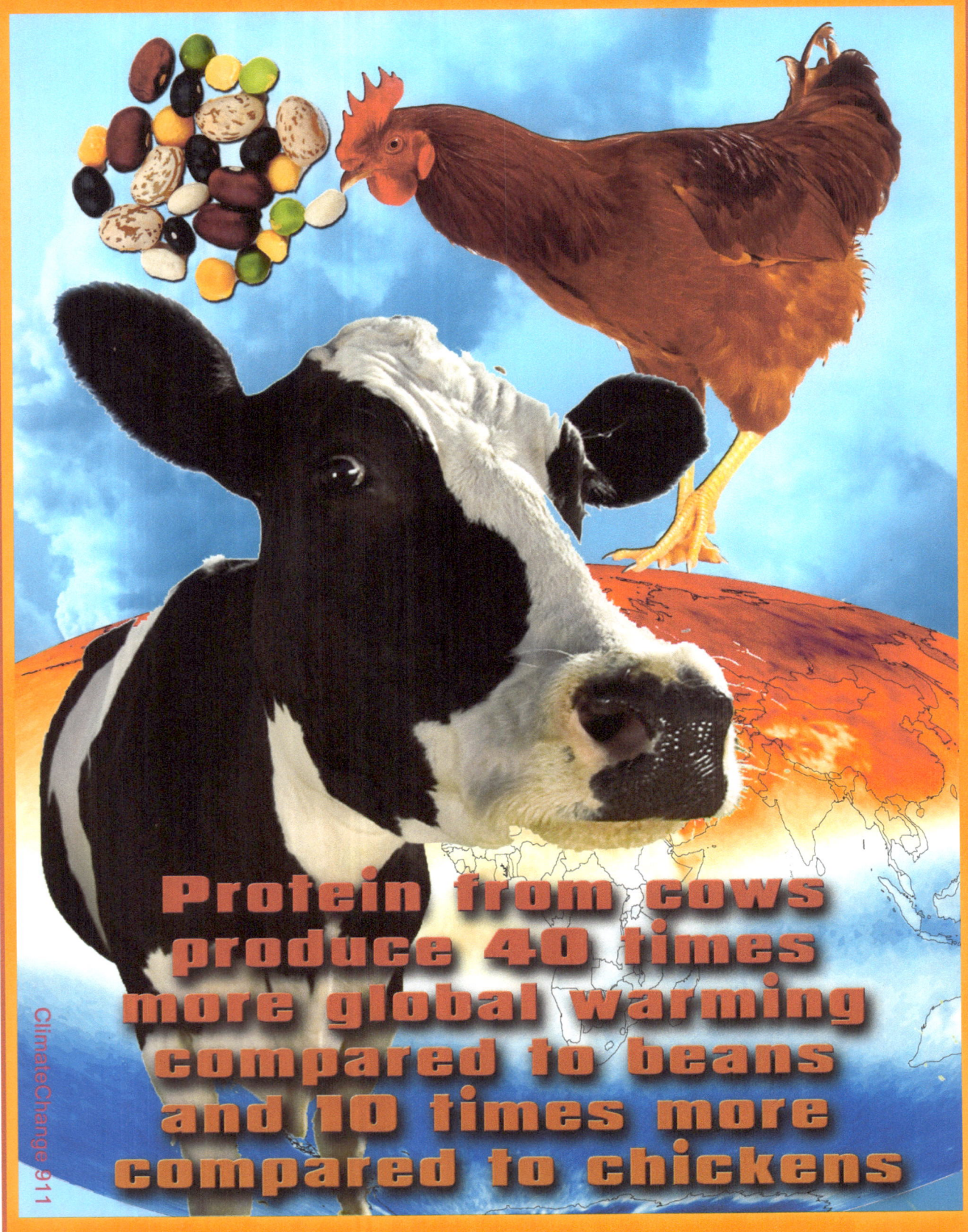

ClimateChange 911

Protein from cows produce 40 times more global warming compared to beans and 10 times more compared to chickens

(*"Meat is 10-40 Times More Warming"*, digital media 2013)

Who's (H)Eating Earth? Memes on Climate, Food & Hope

41

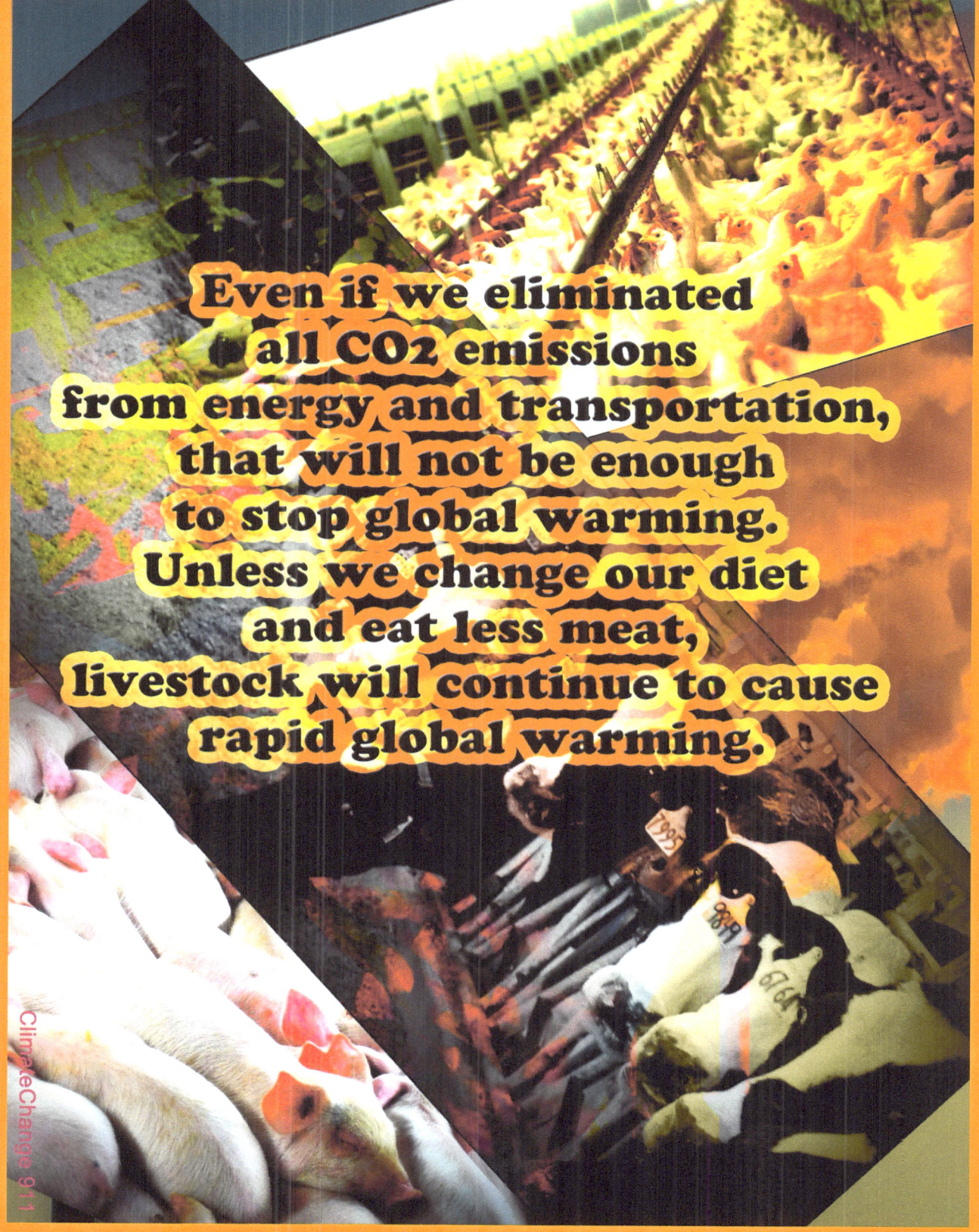

Even if we eliminated
all CO2 emissions
from energy and transportation,
that will not be enough
to stop global warming.
Unless we change our diet
and eat less meat,
livestock will continue to cause
rapid global warming.

("*Impact of Farmed Animals II*", digital media 2013)

Who's (H)Eating Earth? Memes on Climate, Food & Hope

42

GO VEGETARIAN

Save Us From Global Warming!

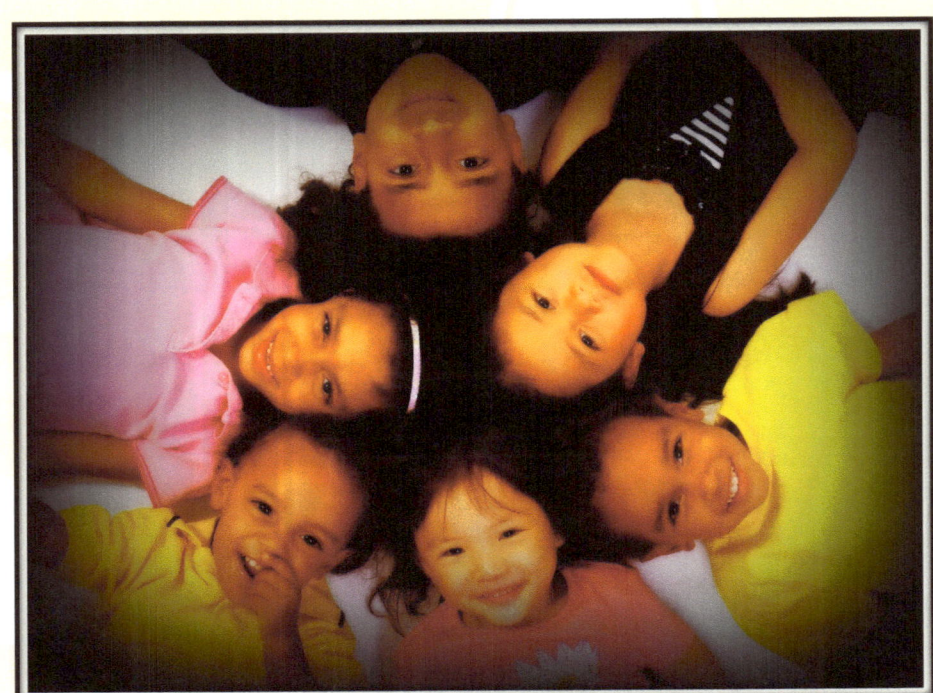

Animal agriculture generates 40% more greenhouse gas than all cars, trucks and planes combined!

For Our FUTURE!

MyLuv4Earth.com

(*"Diet & Children I"*, digital media 2012)

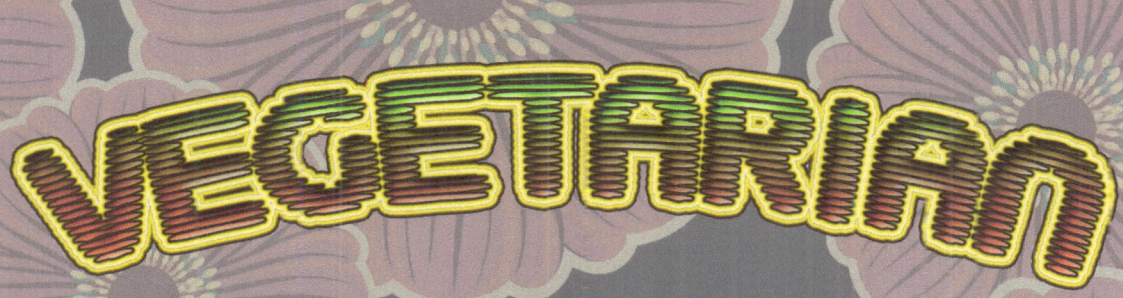

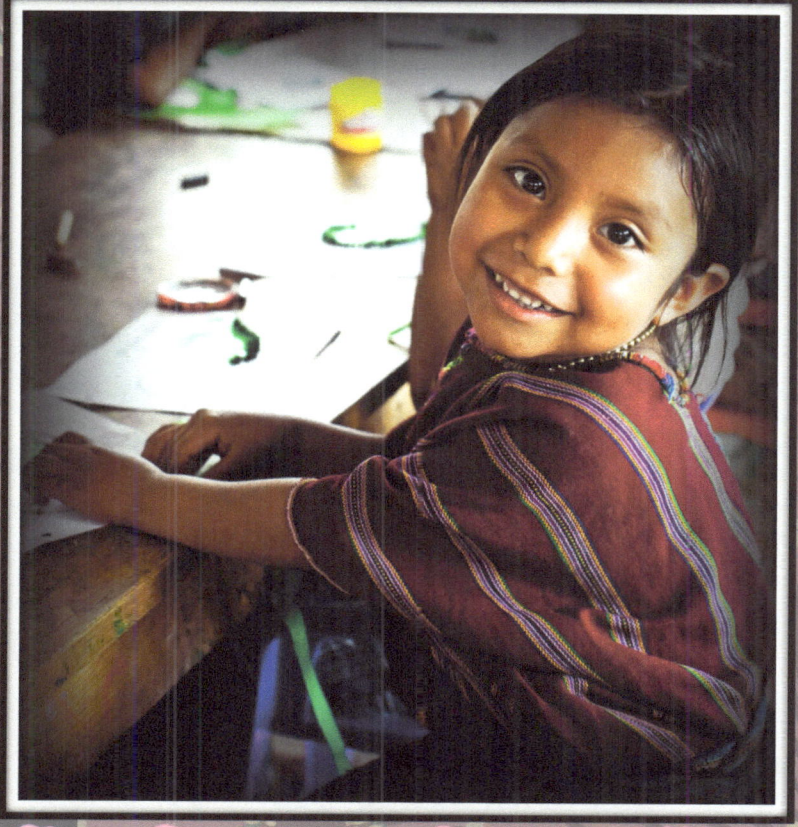

Native American, Aztec & Mayan children in olden times ate 100% vegetarian diets until at least 10 years old

("*Diet & Children II*", digital media 2012)

Who's (H)Eating Earth? Memes on Climate, Food & Hope

44

SOCIETY MUST REDEFINE
ITS RELATIONSHIP
WITH THE SACREDNESS
OF MOTHER EARTH

DECOLONIZE
YOUR
DIET

Climate Change 911

("*Decolonize Your Diet*", digital media 2012)

VEGETARIAN
Cesar Chavez

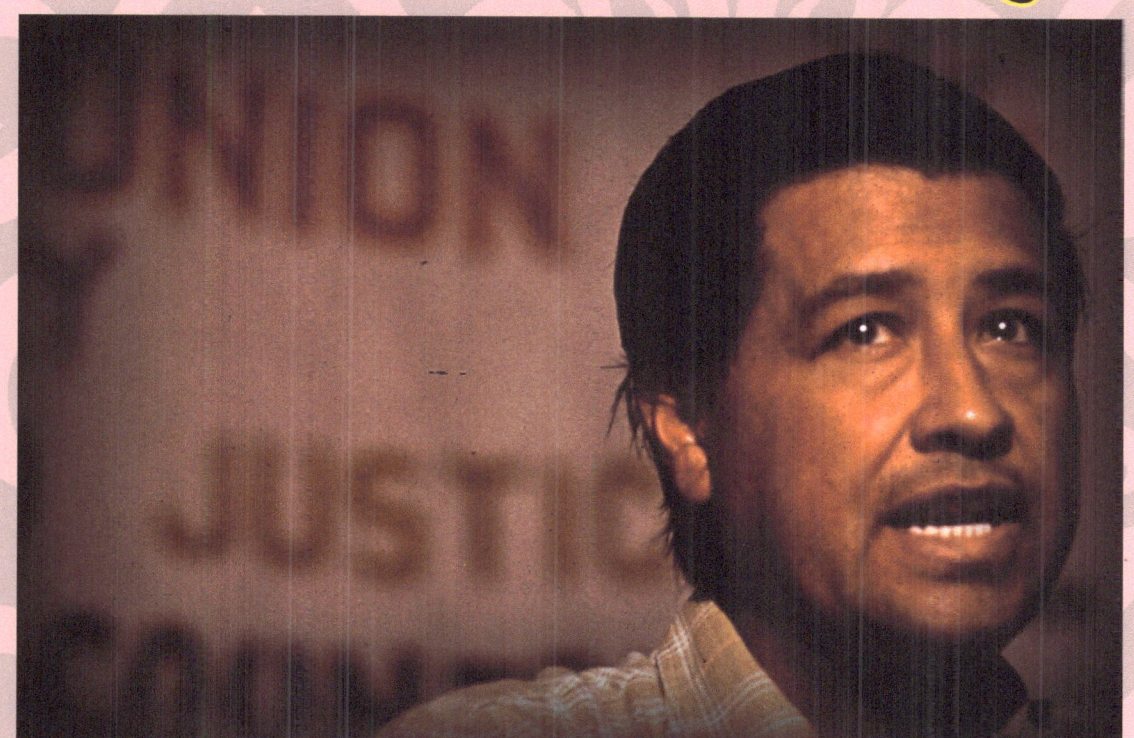

"I became a **vegetarian** after realizing that **animals** feel afraid, cold, hungry and unhappy like we do."

FOR LIFE

Sí, se puede

MyLuv4Earth.com

(*Cesar Chavez: Go Vegetarian for Life*", digital media 2012)

GO VEGAN

Correta Scott King

VEGAN FOR 10 YEARS

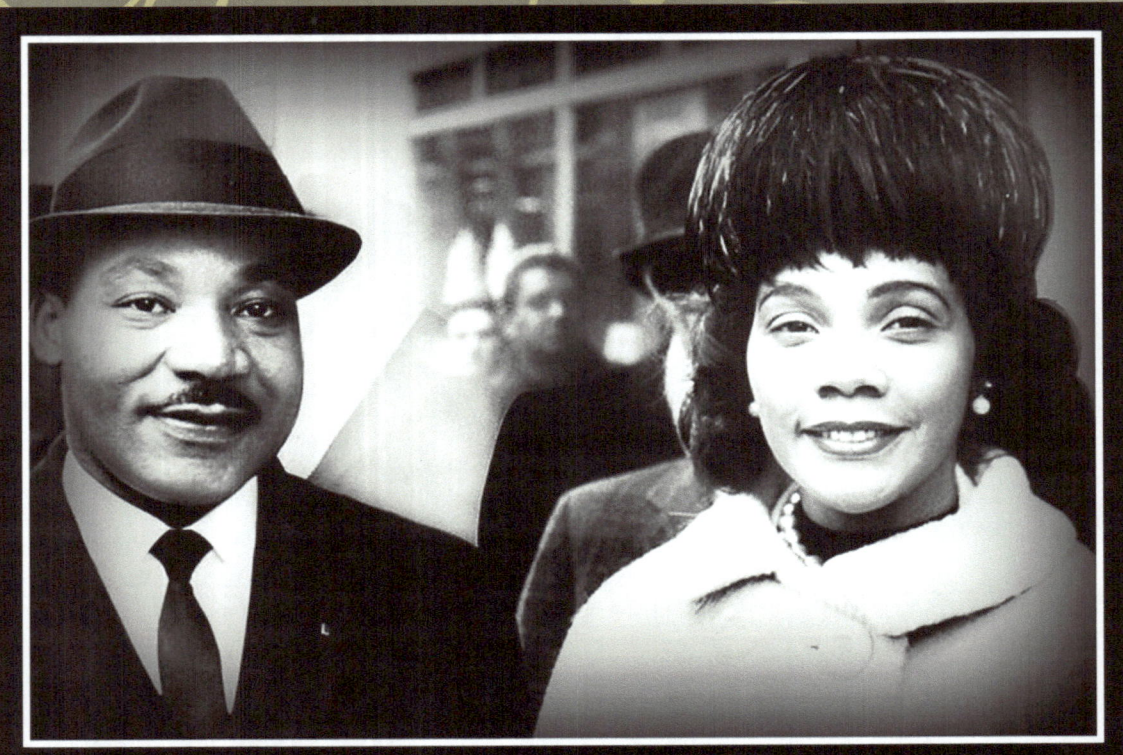

"I prefer to eat mostly Raw or 'Living' foods"

FOR LIFE!

MyLuv4Earth.com

("*Correta Scott King: Go Vegan for Life*", digital media 2012)

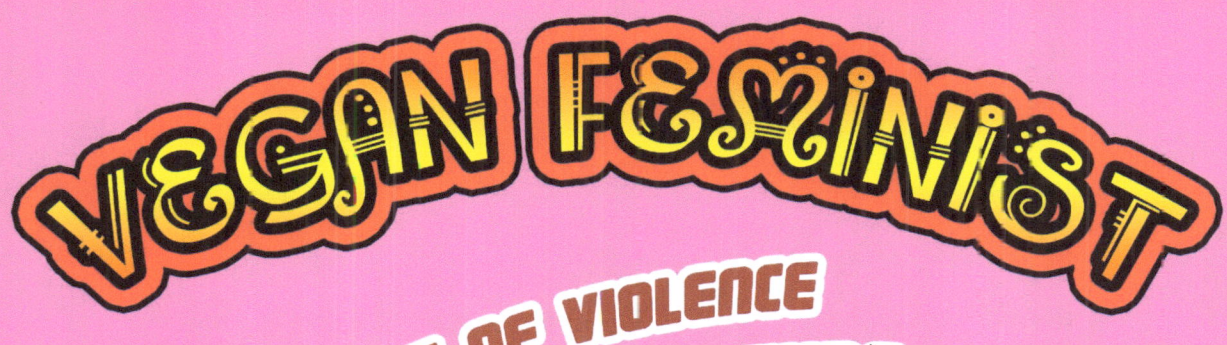

VEGAN FEMINIST

END MALE DIET OF VIOLENCE AGAINST FEMALES AND NATURE!

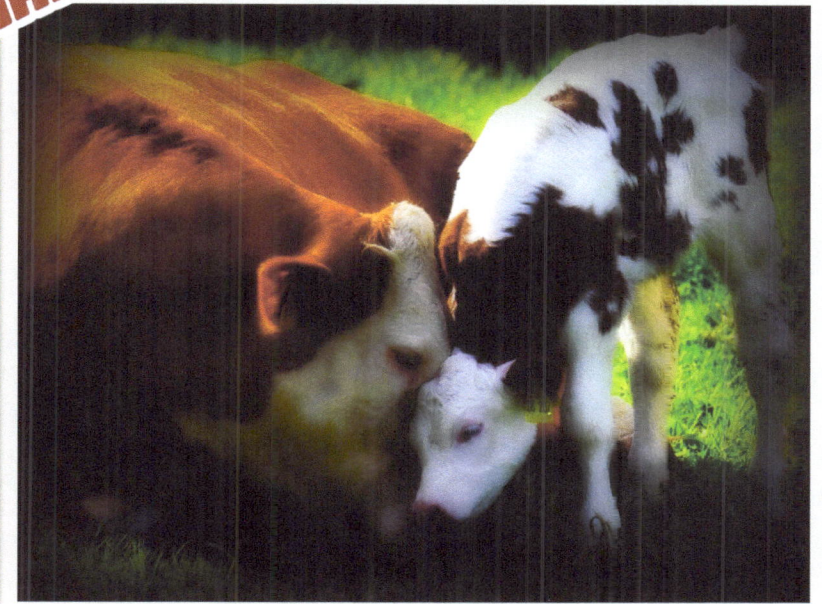

Factory farms Exploit Reproductive Systems! 150 billion Animals KILLED annually!

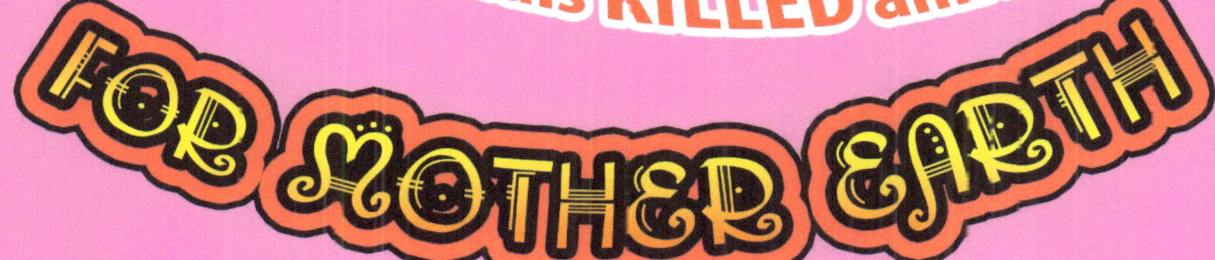

FOR MOTHER EARTH

MyLuv4Earth.com

("*Vegan Feminist for Mother Earth*", digital media 2012)

Who's (H)Eating Earth? Memes on Climate, Food & Hope

48

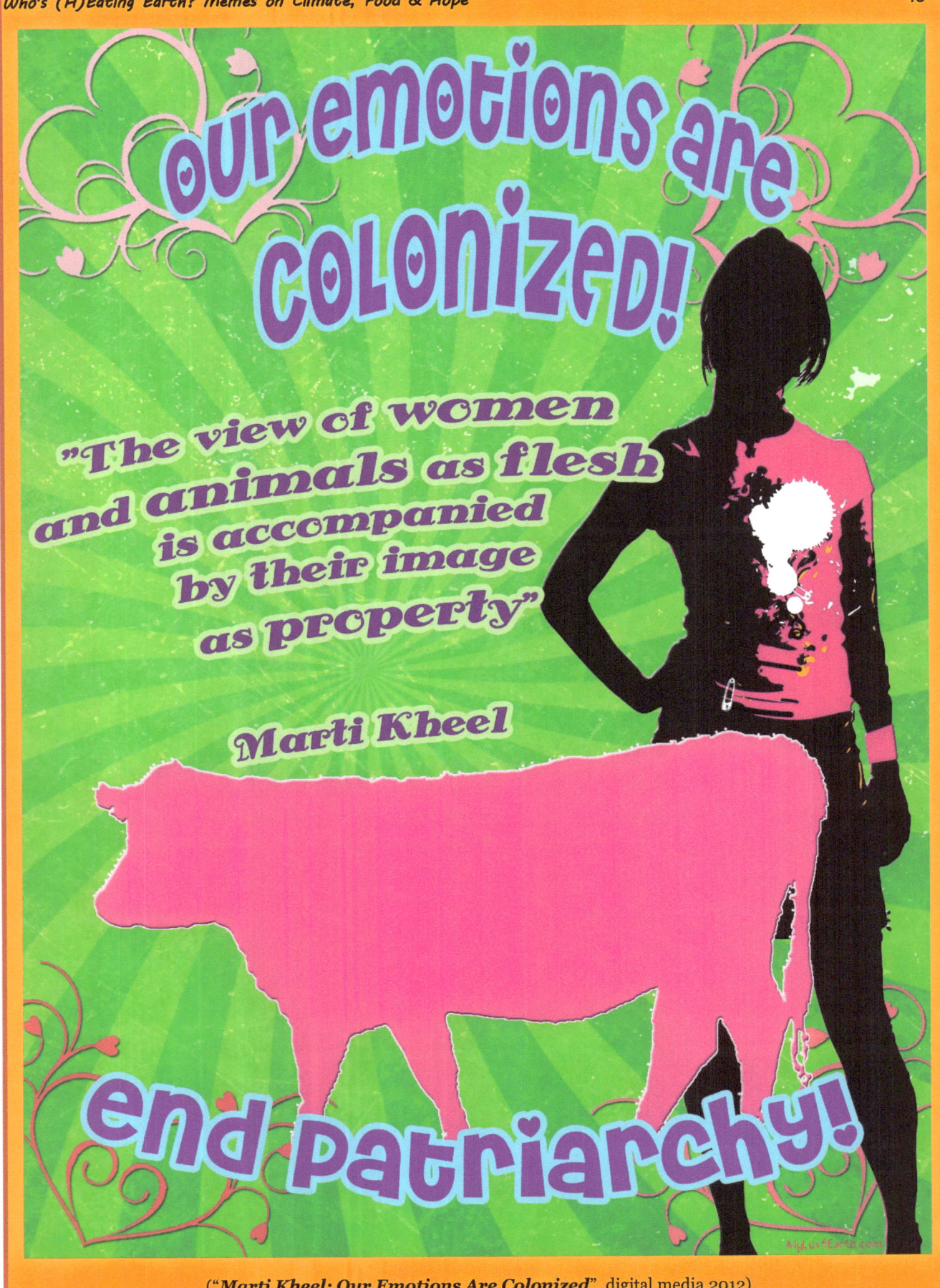

("*Marti Kheel: Our Emotions Are Colonized*", digital media 2012)

healing nature

"Those who contemplate the beauty of the earth find reserves of strength that will endure as long as life lasts"

RACHEL CARSON

" man is a part of nature, and his war against nature is inevitably a war against himself"

is healing ourselves

("*Rachel Carson: Healing Nature is Healing Ourselves*", digital media 2012)

Who's (H)Eating Earth? Memes on Climate, Food & Hope

50

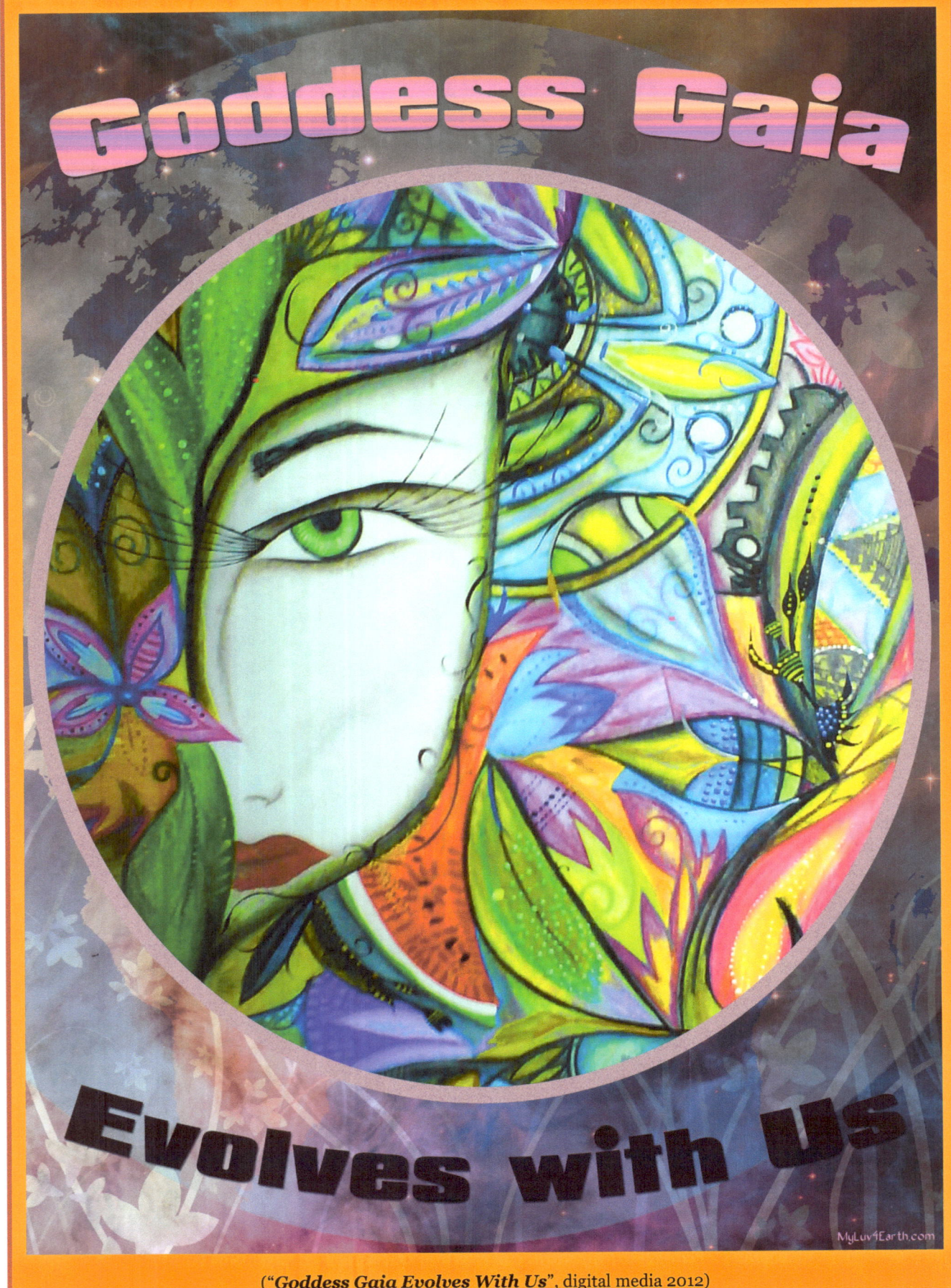

("*Goddess Gaia Evolves With Us*", digital media 2012)

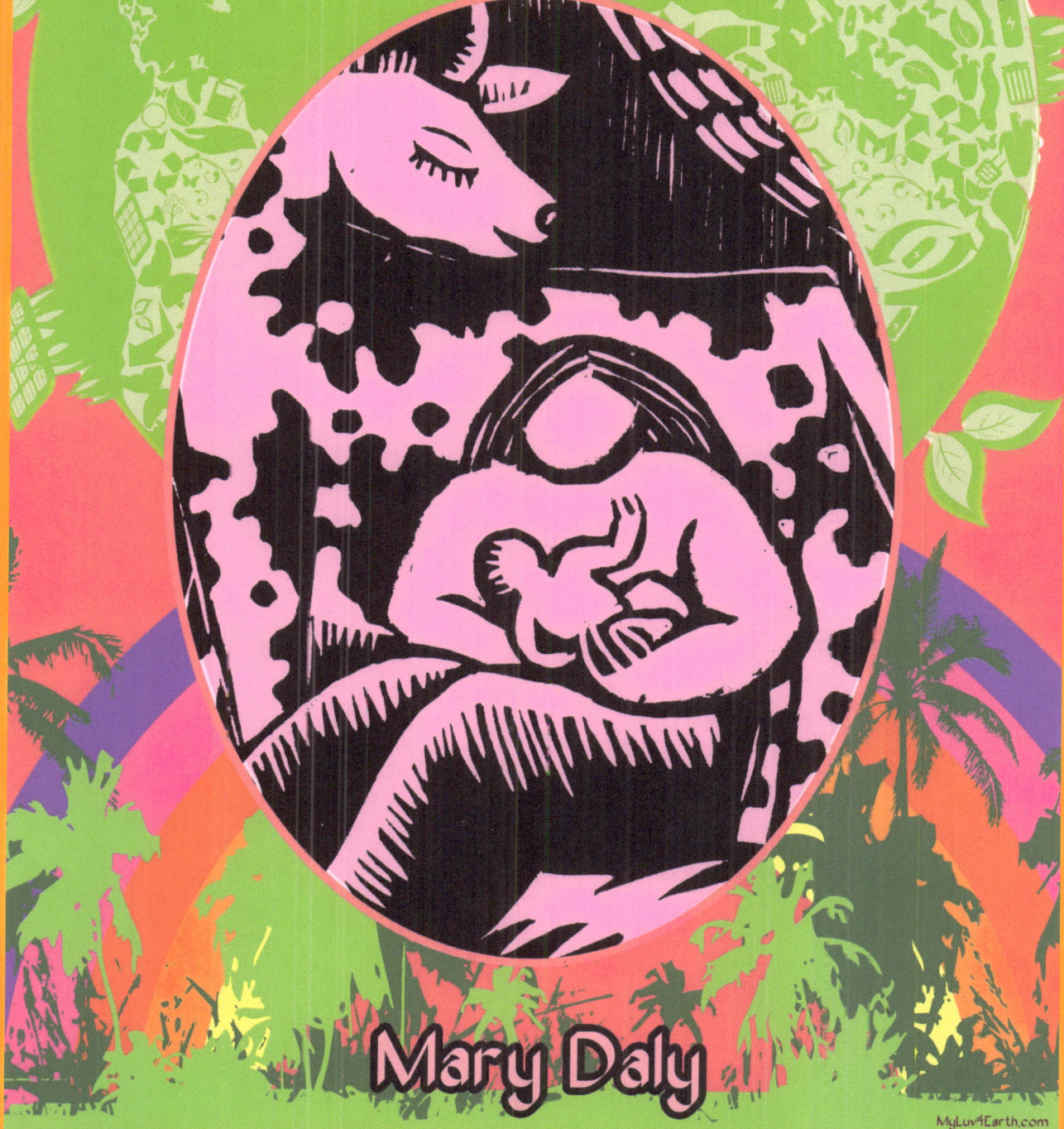

"To care about others, about the earth, to risk our lives for them if necessary – that's what it should be, to be a woman."

Mary Daly

MyLuv4Earth.com

("*Mary Daly – on Gyn/Ecology*", digital media 2012)

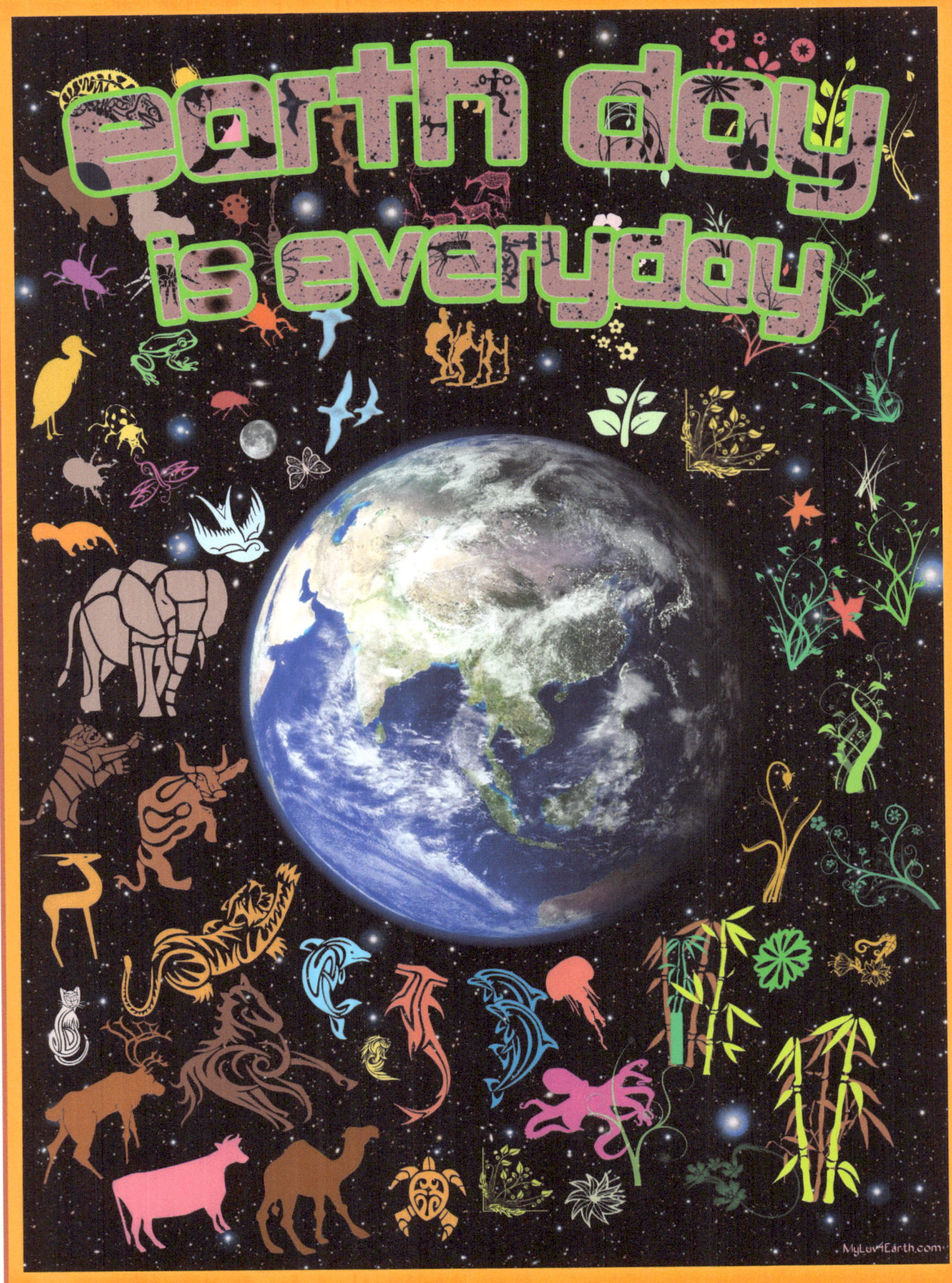

("*Earth Day is Everyday*", digital media 2012)